The Time
of the
Copper Moon

**By
Ragene Henry**

This book is dedicated to Bill,
for always believing
and supporting.

Cover Art by Kathrine Waters

The Time
of the
Copper Moon

Chapter 1

"Why did I ever let Samantha talk me into this?" Libby asked herself for about the hundredth time. She lifted her chin and pulled her shoulders back so far she thought her shoulder blades could touch in back. She swiveled her neck around to check. No, not quite. But Ms. Sullivan would be glad she was working on her posture. She made a skunk face at her reflection in the mirror. "I look like such a dork."

"No, you don't. You look like Big Annie of Calumet," Mom mumbled around the straight pins that stuck out of the corner of her mouth. "Stand still. And straight."

"Still – thrill. Straight – hate – fumigate," Libby grumbled. "Ouch! You poked me."

"Sorry." Mom took another tuck in the back of the thin white gauze of the old fashioned dress. Sticking in her last pin, she popped her head up alongside Libby's in the mirror. "There. That ought to do it."

"Yeah. If only I didn't have to breathe I might even be able to stand it." Libby surveyed herself from the padded white shoulders that made her feel like a Green Bay Packer, to the double rows of ruffles at the dress's hem that tickled the tops of her feet. She could hardly wait to get out of the dress and back into her baggy jeans and hot pink tee shirt with Las Legas sparkling in silver letters that only peeled in a couple of places. That reminded her,

5

she'd better super glue the "V" in Vegas back together before she wore the shirt to school again.

"How are you doing on your Big Annie research?" Mom asked.

"Research – sea perch," Libby said, squeezing her mouth into a fish face. "I wish I'd never let Samantha talk me into this stupid project," she said for about the hundred and first time.

It was all Samantha's fault. And Ms. Sullivan's, too. First Ms. Sullivan announced that everyone who participated in HISTORY ALIVE! was guaranteed an "A" in Social Studies on their report cards. Samantha, who had the biggest collection of "A's" in the world (except for maybe super brain Nathan Westlake), was hooked. On the way home from school she reeled Libby in, too.

"Listen, Libby, have you ever gotten an "A" in Social Studies? Ever?"

"No," Libby had to admit.

"Well, here's your chance. All you have to do is participate in HISTORY ALIVE! You don't even have to study for any tests. Think how happy your mom would be. She might even let you go to the Bad Boyz concert as a reward. Anyhow, it will be fun. Come on, do it with me. Please?"

That night at supper Libby tried to sound casual as she spread butter slowly over her garlic bread. "Mom, what would it be worth to you if I got an "A" in Social Studies on my report card?"

Mom raised an eyebrow. "An 'A'?"

"Yup. A big fat juicy 'A'."

"Hmmmmm…. What would that be worth? A million dollars? A gold medal? A spot on the Oprah show? A heart attack?"

"No, seriously, Mom."

"Seriously, Libby, I would be very happy and very proud."

Libby couldn't remember the last time Mom had said she was proud. Maybe this was her chance.

"Okay," she told Samantha the next day. "I'll do it. I'll join HISTORY ALIVE! with you."

"Yes!" said Samantha. She flapped both her hands in front of her face, fingers spread, fanning her cheeks, elbows bobbing like a chicken gone berserk. "It's going to be so fun. And challenging, too."

That should have been the first clue. Libby should have known that if something was challenging to Samantha, it would be torture to her. But she didn't have a clue what she was in for until she had already gone to the first HISTORY ALIVE! meeting, been conned by Ms. Sullivan, and signed herself up for trouble.

Chapter 2

"Come in, come in. Welcome to HISTORY ALIVE!" chirped Ms. Sullivan. "Samantha, I'm so glad to see you. And Libby….."

"What are you doing here, Libby?" It was Nathan Westlake's sniveling voice. "Didn't anyone tell you this is a G.T. class? Or don't you know what those initials stand for?"

Libby scowled. G.T. class? Nobody had said anything about that. Of course she knew what G.T. stood for, but it had never touched her life before. No one had ever, or would ever, ask her to be in a gifted and talented class. She sent a desperate look toward Samantha, but caught only her back.

"Oh, yeah? I do, too, know what G.T. stands for – gizzards and toads." She stomped away from Nathan, headed for the door. She'd better get out of here before it got really embarrassing.

"Wait. Libby." Cool fingers closed on her upper arm. She spun around, ready to tell Samantha a thing or two. But the cool fingers belonged to the freckled arm of Ms. Sullivan. She yanked her own arm free. "I'm out of here," she said.

But Ms. Sullivan followed her through the door and out into the hall. "Libby, stop right where you are." The no-nonsense teacher voice brought Libby to a halt, but she refused to look up. She would just stare at her Nikes until Ms. Sullivan gave up.

"Why are you leaving?"

Libby shrugged.

Ms. Sullivan grabbed her by both her arms this time. "Libby, I want you to look at me."

Okay, I guess I can look, Libby thought. It's not like she's magic and can put a spell on me and turn me into a cat or something if I look at her face. She looked up. It was just an ordinary face, not a witch's face, not even pretty, with freckles and greenish eyes, and one crooked tooth that slightly overlapped the other, and all surrounded by a halo of frizzy reddish brown hair. Okay. I looked. But I won't talk.

"Tell me. Why are you leaving? I want you to stay." Ms. Sullivan looked squarely into Libby's eyes. She waited, staring without blinking.

"I can't," Libby blurted. "It's a gifted and talented class and I'm not. Gifted. Or talented." She did just put a spell on me, Libby thought. She sucked in a deep breath. At least I didn't meow.

"Who says you're not gifted and talented?"

"Nathan Westlake for one. And just about everybody else in the whole wide world." She'd better stay mad. If she didn't stay mad she might have to cry.

Ms. Sullivan shook her head slowly from side to side. "Libby, I was so happy to see you come to this meeting because you do have gifts and talents, special ones that will be just perfect for HISTORY ALIVE!"

"Oh, yeah? Like what?"

"You have a flare for acting. You have a wonderful creative imagination. You have strong opinions and you aren't afraid to voice them. And you have leadership potential. I think your talents will really make you shine in

HISTORY ALIVE! Please. Come back in. Give it a try?"

Libby hesitated. Could all that be true?

"Who are you going to believe, Nathan or me?" Ms. Sullivan asked.

"Well, when you put it that way...." Libby raised her eyes to the teacher's face. "Okay. I guess I could give it a try."

Ms. Sullivan gave her shoulders a squeeze. "Come on. Let's get this show on the road."

Libby followed Ms. Sullivan back into the room. Meow, she thought. She made a squinty-eyed cat face. "Meow."

"What?" Samantha asked, giving her a puzzled look.

Libby just shrugged.

Chapter 3

Libby found a seat at a desk near the door just in case a quick getaway became necessary. She slouched down into the seat and hunched her shoulders up around her head. Yanking off her glittery silver headband, she combed her fingers through her hair, bringing it down like thick brown curtains on either side of her face.

She watched from under her bangs as Ms. Sullivan strode purposefully to the front of the classroom and started to get the attention of the ten kids buzzing around.

"Okay, ladies and gentlemen," she began. The buzzing lessened. She smiled patiently, waited a moment, and tried again. "Ladies and gentlemen, let's get HISTORY ALIVE! started."

Libby wasn't listening to those words. Instead her brain replayed the words Ms. Sullivan had said out in the hall. She remembered every single one perfectly. "You have a flair for acting," she told herself. "You have a creative imagination. You're not afraid to express your opinions. You have leadership potential. You, Libby Larson, are gifted and talented!" Awesome. She guessed she would have to go around looking gifted and talented from now on.

Libby discovered that she was suddenly sitting up straight. Without realizing it she had pushed the hair out of her face and replaced the silver headband. She looked right at Ms. Sullivan and smiled with all her teeth. "Hey, you guys," she said in her loudest leadership voice, "be quiet. Let's get this show on the road." She gave Ms. Sullivan a big wink. I'm ready, she thought. HISTORY ALIVE! here I come.

But what am I coming to? What is HISTORY ALIVE! all about, anyway? She guessed she'd better start to listen.

*   *   *

"So, what do you think?" Samantha asked as they walked down the sidewalk toward home.

"I don't know. It sounds like a lot of work," Libby replied.

"Yes. If you want to do a good job I guess it will be a lot of work. But I think it will be exciting, too."

Libby shuffled through the leaves at the sidewalk's edge, all brown and crunchy like corn flakes, before you put the milk in. "Do you have any ideas about who you want to be?"

"I have about a hundred possible people," Samantha said.

"Well, when you pick one, maybe you can give me your ninety-nine leftovers because I can't think of anyone."

"That's because you're not really thinking," Samantha retorted. "It's going to be so interesting to find out all about a famous person in history and then make up a costume and write a speech and actually become that character. Well, not actually become, but pretend to be that person. It will be just like being a Hollywood actress."

"Who are you thinking of becoming?" Libby asked,

jumping to the next pile of leaves.

Samantha walked on serenely. "Well, let's see....." She began to number them off on her fingers. "There's Amelia Earhart. I've always been interested in what happened to her and how she tried to fly around the world solo but disappeared."

"Yeah, she'd be cool."

"Or," Samantha put up the second finger. "Susan B. Anthony who worked for women's rights to vote. Or Rosa Parks who wouldn't give up her seat on the bus and helped Black people get their rights. Or Madame Currie. Or maybe a famous actress like Ethel Barrymore or May West. Or Betsy Ross."

"Or Johnny Appleseed!" Libby was getting into the spirit of it now.

"Johnny Appleseed was a man, silly," Samantha reminded her.

"So? If you're a really gifted and talented actress you could act like a man, couldn't you?"

"I guess," Samantha agreed skeptically.

"Or Charlotte Kawbawgum, famous local Native American?" Libby asked with hesitation. "She's not really famous except for here in Marquette County, but I already know a lot about her from my report last spring."

"That's a good idea," Samantha nodded.

Chapter 4

Unfortunately Ms. Sullivan did not think that Charlotte Kawbawgum was a good idea. "Now, Libby, you already know all about Charlotte. You wrote that wonderful report about her last spring. Mrs. Maxim showed it to me. That would not be a challenge. It wouldn't be a learning experience for you."

"I know, but......"

"No buts. In a gifted and talented class we try to challenge ourselves, to stretch our brains. Think of a character that you don't know about, someone you would like to get to know. Stretch, Libby."

Stretch-fetch. Challenge-swallenge, Libby thought. She made a scowling bear face, just so Ms. Sullivan would know she was displeased. But she said, "Okay, I'll try," because she guessed a gifted and talented person would try.

All day long she tried. When she was supposed to be writing her spelling words three times each, she tried. When she was supposed to be doing 187 divided by 42 , she tried. Martha Washington? When she was supposed to be coloring and labeling the planets, she tried. Pocahontas? But none of the names she thought of sparked her interest. And she knew, as sure as she knew her own name, that if she didn't find someone really interesting she would not do a very gifted and talented job on this project.

She asked Mom while she helped make the supper salad. But none of her suggestions made a spark either. Maybe she would just see who Samantha decided on and use one of her leftovers.

But then the phone rang. Libby could tell from Mom's side of the conversation that she was talking to Grandpa Erickson.. "Here, Dad, I'll let you talk to her." She handed the phone to Libby. "Say hi to Grandpa."

Libby really loved Grandpa Erickson. She wished he didn't live so far away. He was much easier to talk to in person.

"Hi, Grandpa. How's the weather in Arizona? Are you staying there for Christmas? Is Grandma getting any better at baking with her bread machine?"

Grandpa chuckled. "Hello. Hotter than blazes. Yes. No."

"What?"

"The weather here in Arizona is hotter than blazes. Yes, we are staying here for Christmas. No, Grandma's bread is still a disaster. Today it tasted like a sponge that had just scrubbed the bathroom floor."

Libby giggled. "You better not let Grandma hear you say that."

"I won't. I promise. I just choke it down, or feed it to the birds when she's not looking. So, how's my girl? How's school going?"

"Oh, let me tell you about HISTORY ALIVE! It's a gifted and talented class and I'm in it. Can you believe it?"

"Of course I can. You are an immensely talented young lady. I wouldn't have any other kind for a granddaughter."

She told Grandpa all about her struggles to find the

right person for HISTORY ALIVE!

"Hmmmmmmm. Let me think for a minute," he said when she had finished. The quiet stretched out until Libby began to squirm. She could picture him standing in the kitchen of the mobile home in the retirement community. He would be staring out the window, squinting his eyes at the bright sun and wrinkling his brow while he thought. Finally he cleared his throat. "Well, one person keeps coming to mind, Libby. Do you remember that I used to work in the copper mines up in the Keweenaw Peninsula?"

"Sure."

"Well, the old timers used to like to talk about the old days and interesting people from the early mining days up there. I heard about this one woman. They called her Big Annie. In fact my father, your great-grandpa Oscar, knew her when he was a young man. She was some sort of hero up there in Calumet when they were trying to start unions for the copper miners. I don't remember too much about her, except that she organized all the women and led parades carrying a big flag. I hear she was real outspoken and wasn't afraid to stand up to people, even the mine managers and the state militia soldiers. I always thought she sounded like an interesting lady."

Libby felt a little tingle between her shoulder blades. Big Annie – fig pannie. A spark lit in the back of her mind. Big Annie, a lady who had opinions and wasn't afraid to speak them!

"Grandpa, you are a genius," she declared. "I just knew I could count on you. I gotta go. I'll let you know what I find out about Big Annie in my research. Bye!"

Chapter 5

"Mom to Libby. Mom to Libby. Come in, Libby," Mom said into Libby's right ear in the mirror's reflection. Or was it her left ear? Is everything backwards in a mirror?

"Ouch! You poked me with a pin again, Mom."

"Sorry, Honey. But at least I got your attention. You were a million miles away. Daydreaming. Or trying to avoid my question."

"What question?"

"I asked how you were doing on your Big Annie research."

"Oh."

"Well? How is it going?"

Libby frowned. "I've learned lots of interesting stuff, but I still have a long way to go. And then I have to put all the facts together into a story that I can tell as if I am Big Annie. An autobiography." She pronounced the word slowly. A gifted and talented word, autobiography, a story someone tells about his own life. Or her own life. "Want to hear what I've learned so far?"

"Sure."

Libby ran to her backpack to get her blue research notebook. She flipped through the first few pages, past the note to Samantha, beyond the drawing of a bird flying over a target on Nathan Westlake's head. She took a big breath and began to read her facts. "Her name was Anne

Clemenc. You say that 'Clem-ents.' She was born in Calumet in 1888, over a hundred years ago. So when I pretend to be Big Annie for History Alive! I'll have to be twenty five years old."

Libby took a breath and continued. "Her parents were George and Mary Klobuchar. They were immigrants from Austria. She married Joseph Clemenc whose family came from Croatia. I had to look that up in an atlas. Croatia is across the Adriatic Sea from Italy. By Yugoslavia." She sucked in another breath as Mom began undoing the buttons down the back of the ruffled white dress. "Her father - George, remember? Well, he worked in the copper mines for thirty years. And her mother.....?" Libby raised a quizzing eyebrow at her mom.

"Mary," Mom replied.

Libby grinned. "Yes. Mary. She worked for rich people doing their laundry and being a maid. They were very poor."

"Really? With both of them working and him with a good job in the mines, still they were very poor?"

"Listen, Mom. The mines were different in the olden days. They didn't pay good wages. And the working conditions were terrible. I read that every week one worker died. And every day two men got crippled. It was not a great place to work. Anyhow, Annie's job was working for the church, helping the crippled miners. She also took in laundry. I wouldn't like to do that. The laundry, I mean. They didn't even have washers and dryers back then."

"Arms up, Libby."

Libby raised her arms so Mom could pull the dress up over her head. "Oooh, that feels much better. Now I can breathe. "She filled up her lungs until her chest stuck out, then foofed the breath out and upward, lifting her bangs.

"So, that's one of the things that made Annie so angry."

"Doing laundry?"

"No, Mom. You are not paying attention. The dead and crippled miners. So when the miners went on strike to get better wages and working conditions, she decided to help them."

"How could she help?"

"Well, she organized all the women and children and they had parades at the crack of dawn every morning, down the main street, past the mines and the mine manager's house. Annie led the parades. She always carried a huge flag on a ten foot pole."

"Is that why they called her 'Big Annie'?"

"Nope. Are there any Oreo cookies left? I'm starving."

"Libby, why was she called 'Big Annie'?"

"Because she was six feet, two inches tall. The newspaper reporters gave her that name. She got to be famous in newspapers all over the country. I just got to that part in my research. The last story I read was from one of those newspapers. It told about a time when soldiers on horses cut Annie's flag and threatened her, but Annie didn't back down. She was a hero in all the newspapers." Libby put her hands on her hips. "Cookies, Mom?"

Mom crooked her finger and Libby followed her to the kitchen and the Oreos. There, propped inside the back door where Mr. Formolo, the mailman, always put their packages, sat a bulging tan envelope addressed to Miss Libby Larson.

Chapter 6

"A package! Look, Mom, it's for me!" Libby dashed to
the package and swooped it up. "It's from Arizona. From
Grandpa. See? The sticker says 'Martin G. Erickson.'
And it's not even my birthday. I wonder what it could be."
She began ripping at the envelope's flap. "Oh, cool.
Bubble wrap." Libby stopped in the middle of unfolding the
small rectangle to pop a few plastic bubbles between her
fingers. She loved bubble wrap. Somehow it made her
feel powerful and happy, as if each loud pop of air pumped
up her happiness thermometer one degree.

"The bubble wrap is not the present, Libby," Mom
reminded her. "Let's see what's inside."

"Oh, yeah." Libby continued to unfold the layers of
plastic, saving the bubbles for later. When the last layer
was lifted she saw, gleaming up at her, a leaf made of
copper pinned onto an index note card.

"Libby," she read from Grandpa's printing on the card.
"I found this pin in a box of my father's special things. I
don't know why it was special to him, but it reminded me
of you and your Big Annie project at school. Could you
use it on your costume? Keep it as a family souvenir. It's
an antique! Love, Grandpa E."

Libby unpinned the leaf from the card. She turned it
over and over in her hand. The metal felt warm and
strangely soft on her palm. It was beautiful, a softly

gleaming sliver of copper, about an inch across, shaped like a baby birch leaf. She turned it over and saw something etched on the back of the pin. It looked like letters. She brought it over to the window to see better. Yes. It was letters. It looked like OELAK. Oelak? What in the world did that spell? She knew her great grandfather was Swedish. Maybe it was a word in the Swedish language. Right now she didn't know and didn't care. It was beautiful and Grandpa had given it to her. "Cool," Libby whispered. "Cool – rule. Pin – twin. Copper – topper – tear dropper." She didn't understand why, but suddenly a sad, melancholy feeling washed over her and she felt she might burst into tears. That was crazy. She was happy. Very excited to get this present. She shook her head and as quickly as it had come, the sadness left.

"This will be so cool on my dress," she said. She touched the pin to the chest of her pink Las Legas tee-shirt. Nope. It definitely needed to be on the dress, not the tee-shirt. Tomorrow, at school, when they had to try on their costumes and get everything okayed by Ms. Sullivan, she would pin the copper leaf onto one of the pleats that ran down the dress front. Oh yes, it would be cool-rule. But in the meantime she would find the glue and glue the "V" in Vegas back together on her tee shirt.

*   *   *

"Your Sacagawea costume is great, Samantha. I love all the beads." Libby ran her fingers through the beaded fringe across the front of Samantha's brown dress. It reminded her of her Ojibwa friend Charlotte. She sighed. Charlotte was from another time, a strange and mysterious encounter, and Libby knew she would never see her again. She tried to pull her thoughts back from

26

the past to concentrate on what Samantha was saying.

"I like your Big Annie dress, too." Samantha paused and tapped her index finger on her lower lip. "You know, I don't think I've ever seen you in a dress before."

"That's because I hate dresses." Libby made a twitchy rabbit face. "Can you imagine in the olden days girls had to wear dresses all the time? How could they breathe? Or run? Or ride bikes?"

Samantha straightened the feathered and beaded clasp decorating her long dark brown braid. "What are you going to do with your hair? Do you know how Big Annie's hair looked?"

"Yes. Her picture was in all the newspapers. Even in Detroit and Chicago and New York. But they were all the same picture. She parted her hair in the middle and pulled it back and put it in some sort of knot or clump on the back of her head. She had a sweet smile. Like this." Libby had been practicing her Annie smile, not too wide, just showing the bottom half of her top teeth. She tested it on Samantha. "How's this?"

"About as sweet as a dill pickle."

Libby exchanged her sweet Annie smile for a sour pickle face so Samantha could see the difference. Then she raced on, "Wait 'til you see what my grandpa sent me. It's the perfect thing for my costume and it even came from the olden days in the Copper Country, from my great-grandfather." Libby pulled her hand out from the pocket hidden deep within the folds of the white dress. "Look," she commanded, opening her fist to reveal the copper leaf pin.

"Oooooh! It's beautiful, Lib. Let's see where it should go." Samantha snatched the pin from Libby's palm. Libby wasn't sure she wanted anyone else touching it, but she squeezed her lips together and said nothing.

Samantha held the pin up to the pleats on Libby's dress, first on the right and then on the left side of her chest. She held it up to the dress's collar, first on the right and then on the left side. She shrugged. "I can't decide. It looks good anywhere."

Libby reached for the pin, happy to feel its warmth again in her own hand. "I'll have to check in a mirror," she decided. She turned from Samantha and called out to the teacher, "Ms. Sullivan, can I go to the bathroom to check in a mirror for where my copper pin should go?"

Ms. Sullivan came up close enough to see the gleaming slice of copper on Libby's palm. "That's beautiful, Libby. It's the perfect thing to finish off your costume. We'll need to put your hair up." She put both hands to Libby's hair, pulled it back and twisted. She held the knotted hair back with her left hand, leaned backward and surveyed Libby. She reached back into her own hair with her right hand and pulled out several hair pins. She put them between her lips just as Mom had with the sewing pins. Then, one at a time, she poked them into Libby's hair. Libby felt them scrape along her scalp at the back of her head.

"There," Miss Sullivan said.

Libby tried her sweet half-teeth Annie smile. Ms. Sullivan smiled back. "You look just like Big Annie. There's only one more thing you need."

"What?"

"Well, think, Libby. What was Big Annie famous for? What did she do?"

Libby knew that a gifted and talented person would be able to answer that question in a heartbeat. Ba-boom. Ba-boom. It took two heartbeats, but Libby had the answer. "A flag. A big, humongous flag. On a pole. So I could lead.....I mean so Annie could lead the parades."

"I think I might know where you can find one," Ms. Sullivan said. "Behind the stage in the auditorium, in the corner, there's a narrow set of metal stairs. If you go carefully up those stairs you'll find a storeroom where we keep old scenery and props and Christmas trees and stuff. Over in the back corner, on the right side, I think there's an old flag on a pole, just leaning there, waiting for you. Nathan Westlake is going up there to find a sword for his Benedict Arnold costume. Go with him. But be careful."

Libby's eyes opened wide. A secret storage room in the school that no one knew existed. Well, not kids, anyway. Full of interesting old stuff. She would be the first to explore it. It would be such an exciting adventure. But, wait a minute. Go up to a dark, spooky room full of cobwebs and creepy shapes and scary shadows, just her and Nathan Westlake? She didn't like the sound of that.

Chapter 7

"C'mon, Beans-for-brains. Let's go." Nathan Westlake crooked a finger at Libby.

Libby made a toad face and followed him down the hall. She thought he looked silly in pants that ended at the knees and tall ribbed socks. From the back she could see his big ears sticking out of his red hair on either side of his head. It seemed like she mostly saw the back of him. He was always rushing to be first in line for anything. And he sat two seats ahead of her in class. If she could see the front of him she knew she'd see a face full of freckles. Someday she'd get close enough to him to count them. She bet he had five thousand freckles.

The baggy sleeves of his white shirt flapped around his skinny arms as he hustled ahead of her. He walked fast, just fast enough so Libby couldn't catch up, so they'd never come even, so he'd reach the secret storage room first. She was just plain old tired of him being first at everything. Not this time, Big Brain, she thought. She put her feet into high gear and launched herself into a strong run. Before Nathan realized it, she was even with him. He looked at her in surprise and planted his back foot. Libby could tell he was shifting into high gear and about to run, too. So she shoved her weight sideways into him, sending him bumping, off balance, into the auditorium doorframe.

Libby took advantage of his stumble and raced to the front of the auditorium, bounded up onto the stage, found the metal stairs in the back corner, and scrambled up into the darkness at the top. She could hear Nathan's shoes pounding on the first metal stairs. Her hand groped along the wall searching for a light switch. Nathan's heavy breathing sounded closer behind her. "I'll get you for that, Bean-brain. You'll pay."

Libby suddenly realized she did not want to tangle with him all alone in the dark, too far away for anyone to hear a cry or a call for help. In her mind his muscles grew bigger and stronger each second. There was only one thing to do. Libby thought of it just at the moment when her hand found the light switch. She flipped it. A single hanging light bulb gave a dim orangey glow to the storage room.

Apology. That was her idea. "I'm sorry, Nathan. I didn't hurt you, did I?"

"You? Hurt me? Ha!" He stuck out his hands, palms toward Libby, and gave her a shove. Libby stumbled backwards into a metal shelf. "There. How does that feel, Bean-brain?"

"Not so good," Libby admitted, rubbing her scraped elbow. "OK. We're even," she said hopefully.

Nathan seemed to have forgotten all about it. "Wow! Look at all the junk," he said. "How am I ever going to find a sword in this mess? Somebody should clean this place up and get it organized."

"Organized-snorganized," Libby mumbled. She gave her elbow one last squeeze and headed for the back corner, on the right side. Sure enough, there it was. Wrapped around a pole that was taller than Libby, the old flag leaned in the corner, waiting for her, just like Ms.

Sullivan had said. She picked the pole up and holding it out in front of her, turned it in her hands, unwrapping the flag. She held the blue square out and counted the stars. Eight in each row. Six rows. Eight times six equals 48. Forty eight stars – a flag from before Hawaii and Alaska became states. She wondered how old the flag was and how many stars there had been on the flag in Big Annie's day. Something else I'll have to find out in my research, she thought. She let go of the blue and the flag fell into folds around the pole. She held the pole straight up like Big Annie would have and marched a few steps, waving the flag slightly from side to side in the narrow passage between stacked boxes.

Out of the corner of her eye she saw a flash of red and white over her right shoulder. She pinched her eyebrows together, turned, and walked toward it. A mirror! Just what she needed. An old fashioned, full length mirror on a stand. She touched her fingers to the glass and the mirror wobbled on its stand. When she drew her hand back she could see her fingerprints shining through the dust. She propped the flagpole against the mirror's stand, held onto the edge and wiped her hand across the glass, back and forth like a windshield wiper. Now she could see her reflection in the dark wavery glass.

She reached into her dress pocket again and pulled out the copper leaf pin. She held it up to the pleats on the right side of her chest, all the while staring at her reflection in the old mirror. Her chest felt warm. In the mirror her eyes traveled up from the warmth of the pin to her face, to her eyes. She stared. "What?" she whispered. Her eyes looked different, not like the eyes she saw everyday in the bathroom mirror. She looked away. It must just be this old mirror, she thought. Or some trick of light. Her hand fell to her side and she

looked again into her reflected eyes. How silly. Of
course they were her eyes. Who else's could they be?
    She glanced down at her fingers as she lifted the pin
up to the pleats on the left side of her chest. The warmth
suffused her once more. She peered at her reflection
again. She blinked. The eyes were strange again. Not
like her own. But eyes she had seen before.
Somewhere.
    Despite the warmth in her chest Libby felt a shiver
travel up her spine. She looked again at the eyes in the
mirror and felt a strange sadness wash over her. "What?"
she said aloud. What was it about this pin? She had had
the same feeling before but she couldn't remember when.
She felt dizzy and closed her eyes. Both arms fell to her
sides. "Take a deep breath, Libby," she told herself. "Get
a grip. You're letting this place spook you out." She took
three deep breaths, letting each one out slowly.
    She opened her eyes again, hands at her sides.
Staring straight into her reflected face, she brought the
pin slowly up to her chest. Yes! There was a change, a
hazy difference. She moved her arm out from her body,
held it straight out from her side, outside the mirror's
reflection. Take a breath, she reminded herself. Yes, a
whole different feeling. Bring the pin back into the chest.
Feel the change, the warm dizziness creeping over her.
Hold it out. Take a breath. In. Out. Changing eyes.
Warm. Cold. Dizzy. "Something is very strange here,"
she said aloud.
    Nathan Westlake had come up behind her. He leaned
and she could see his face reflected beside hers. "Yeah,"
he said, "it's you. You're very strange." He grabbed for
the flag. "What's this? I could use this."
    "No, you can't. It's mine! It's Annie's!" Libby lunged
for the flag, trying to wrest it from him. Nathan held onto

the pole, gripping it hard with his Popeye muscles.

Libby grabbed the edge of the flag. She tugged but couldn't budge it from Nathan's grasp. "Let go!" she screamed at him.

"Make me, Bean-brain." His laugh made Libby even angrier. She made her most ferocious pit bull face and turned herself quickly, wrapping the flag over her left shoulder. If she kept twirling maybe she could wrap herself completely into the flag like a pig-in-a-blanket. Then Nathan would let go of the pole. Her right hand still clasped the pin. It pressed against her chest as she made one complete rotation, wrapping herself in the flag. She kept turning. Facing the mirror again she saw the strange ghostly eyes staring out at her once more.

"Hey," Nathan yelled when he realized what she was doing. "Cut that out." He grabbed at Libby, trying to unwrap the flag from around her. She tried to back away from him. But she forgot that she would not be able to move her wrapped up legs. She started to lose her balance, started to fall backward. She felt Nathan's weight crashing into her. A hot sharpness stabbed into her chest. The pin, she thought. "Agh-h-h."

She could not stop herself from falling and neither could Nathan. They fell together in a tangled heap of boy, girl, and flag, crashing into the old mirror. Glass shattered; wood cracked. Red and white stripes covered Libby's face and the last thing she remembered were the ghostly eyes in the mirror.

Chapter 8

"Ow! Get off me," Libby moaned. Trapped in the cocoon of the flag she couldn't budge Nathan's weight. She could see him lying crosswise over the top of her, hands still clutching the flagpole. But he didn't answer. "Nathan?" No response. She twisted around until she freed her head from the flag. She could see Nathan's face. His eyes remained closed, "Oh, my gosh. You better not be dead, Nathan Westlake."

She managed to bend her knees enough to jostle Nathan. He groaned and Libby breathed a sigh of relief. She watched for his eyes to open and soon they began to flutter. She tried again. "Nathan, get off me."

He rubbed his eyes and looked at her with a puzzled expression. Then he remembered the flag wrestling and the fall. He unclasped the flagpole and pushed himself off Libby. "At least I had a soft landing," he said. He knelt beside her flag cocoon, grinning. "You look pretty funny."

"Funny – runny – 911-y," Libby grumbled. Then a change washed over Nathan's face. The smart-alecky grin disappeared. He replaced it with a look of dazed puzzlement.

"What the heck?" His glance flitted around them from side to side. He shook his head as if to clear the cob webs out. "Something is very weird here, Libby," he said.

37

Libby figured whatever it was must be truly weird for Nathan to call her by her name instead of Bean-brain.

"What's the matter?"

"Look around you."

"I would if I could. Help me get out of this flag. Unroll me or something."

Nathan helped her roll free of the flag. She heard a pinging sound and looked down in time to see her copper leaf pin land on the wooden boards on which she stood. She bent down to pick it up and quickly fastened it onto the pleats on her dress front. This time she didn't even think about what side it should go on. She pinned it on her left, near her heart, right where she'd felt the sharp pain before they fell. She gathered the flag up in her arms and held onto the pole so he couldn't grab it again. Only after she had secure possession of the flag did she take time to look around.

The mirror was gone. The metal shelves and stacked boxes were gone. The storage room was gone. The whole school had disappeared! They were outside, on a wooden sidewalk. Wooden sidewalk? Libby looked closer at her surroundings.

It was a wooden sidewalk. Weathered planks marched one after the other down to the corner on her right and up to the corner on her left. They were outside in some sort of town. An old fashioned town. The board sidewalk connected two story brick or wooden buildings with narrow windows and fancy trims and moldings.

The building right in front of them had a bay window sticking out in the middle of the second story. The wooden building was painted a pale green, trimmed in gold. Libby tried to remember all the colors of green in her sixty-four crayon box. Spring green? Blue green? Yellow green? Spruce green? Asparagus green? That was it. The store front was asparagus green. Green and gold strips of wood separated the first and second floors. On the first floor there were two doors in a center alcove. Two businesses, or offices. Large glass windows displayed cupboards filled with strange objects, tools and bottles and cans. Above each window hung large green signs. Libby read the fancy gold lettering on the left sign. "Simon Westerberg, M.D." and underneath that, "Physician and Surgeon." The sign on the right side said, "Cyrus Westerberg, D.D.S. " and underneath, "Family Dentist."

"Look, Nathan. " She pointed up at the signs. "I bet they're brothers."

Nathan still wore the strange puzzled expression. "I don't get it," he said. "One minute we're in a storeroom at school. The next minute we're outside in this place, wherever this place is."

Wherever this place was, it was cold. A wintery wind pushed Libby's long skirt against her legs. She shivered and crossed her arms, rubbing her hands up and down her sleeves.

"Burrrr," Nathan said. "I'm freezing."

"Double burr," Libby added.

Libby gazed farther up the street. Across the road and on the next corner a big three story brick building stood proudly, with windows all across the front. Vertin's Department Store, the sign said. Libby walked several paces until she could make out what was in the windows. Mannequins – ladies, men and children, dressed in very old-fashioned clothes. The male mannequins wore dark suits with high white collars and round topped black hats. The women wore long dresses trimmed with ruffles and beads. They carried boxes wrapped in gold paper and tied with big red bows. The children looked, Libby thought, sort of like she and Nathan looked in their

History Alive! costumes-girls wore long dresses, boys wore knee length pants and tall socks. "Hmmmmm. Interesting," she murmured.

She returned to where Nathan still sat on the wooden sidewalk looking dazed.

"What's going on, Libby?" he asked, looking up at her as she walked past him.

"I'm not sure," she said. She clomped down the sidewalk toward the other corner. As she neared it she saw a big stone building shining in gold and orange and brown sitting regally, like the queen of buildings on the opposite corner. It had a fancy entrance with brick arches and wide steps. A marquee announced that it was the Calumet Opera House.

Calumet? Wooden sidewalks? Old-fashioned clothes? Could it be? Could it have happened again? Could she and Nathan have somehow, magically and mysteriously traveled through time to Big Annie's town? She needed to find out what year it was.

She returned again to Nathan. "I don't know if you are going to believe this or not, Nathan, but I think we may have traveled back in time when we fell through the mirror. I think we are in Calumet, Big Annie's town, in the past."

Nathan looked up at her, squinting. He curled his lip and gave her a disgusted look. "That's impossible, Bean-brain. You don't actually believe it's possible to travel through time, do you? That's the stupidest thing I've ever heard."

Libby sat down on the boards again, facing Nathan. She sat cross-legged and pulled her white skirt over them. She looked Nathan right in the eye with her most solemn wise – owl look. "Yes, I do believe in time travel. This isn't the first time it has happened to me.

40

Remember when we were studying Michigan history and the discovery of iron ore last spring?"

Nathan nodded.

"Well, it happened then. I fell off the monument at Miners' Park and when I woke up I was back in 1845. I met Charlotte Kawbawgum and her father, Chief Marji Gesick. I was there when he led the mining men to the shining rocks. That's how I knew so much for my report."

"Sure you were there," Nathan said, laughing. "And I was with the Easter Bunny delivering eggs. Oh, and with the tooth fairy collecting teeth."

"Honest, Nathan. You know I'm not smart enough to make all that up."

"That part's true." Nathan shook his head. "But the rest is just ...."

He stopped in mid-sentence. Bang! A door slammed behind them and a raggedy man stumbled forward from the dentist's door. He held a hand to his jaw and mumbled.

"Sir?" Libby stood up and called to him. He paused and stopped his mumbling to look at her. "What year is this?"

The man made a harumphing noise and shook his head. "I don't know what they're teaching children in that there school if they don't even know what year it is." He shook his head sadly and stumbled off down the street.

"The year?" A deep voice behind her said. "Why, it's 1913. December month. What are you two children doing out in the cold with no coats? Come in to my office and warm up."

"1913?" Nathan repeated, dazed. He looked at Libby. "This is starting to freak me out," he said quietly. She nodded solemnly. They followed Dr. Cyrus Westerberg, D.D.S., Family Dentist, into his office.

Chapter 9

"What are you two children doing outside in December without winter coats?" Dr. Cyrus Westerberg asked again.

Libby looked a long way up to find dark blue eyes staring seriously down at her, waiting for a reply. What could they possibly answer to his question? That they didn't have coats? That they hadn't known it was December? That they didn't know what they were doing here? A gifted and talented person would be able to think of some sort of answer. Libby sent a desperate look toward Nathan. Nathan stared at his feet. He wouldn't meet her eyes, let alone the penetrating blue ones of Dr. Cyrus Westerberg, DDS, Family Dentist. What good was it to have such a big brain if it couldn't help you think fast in an emergency? "Well, sir, " she began, "I, uh, I mean, we... we, um, were supposed to meet my uncle......." Her voice trailed off.

"Your uncle? Who would that be? Perhaps I know him."

"He works in the mines." The sentence just popped from her mouth. It was the only thing Libby could think of that might make sense. If they really were in the past, in Calumet in 1913, most men would work in the mines.

Dr. Cyrus Westerberg moved slowly toward a black iron stove. He opened a door on the front. Libby could see a red hot glow inside the stove's belly. He gave the hot coals a stir with a long metal rod. Then, reaching down to a crate on the floor, he picked up a piece of wood in each large hand, shoved them into the stove, and jammed the door shut again. "Come closer to the stove and get some warmth," he ordered Libby and Nathan.

They moved gratefully toward the heat. Libby stretched her hands out closer and rubbed her palms together, hoping the doctor wouldn't ask any more questions. But her heart sank as he started right up where he left off. "What's your uncle's name?"

Libby's heart pounded in her chest. Name? What name? Think, brain. Her gaze fell on the copper leaf pin on her chest. "Oscar," she said, remembering her great-grandfather's name. "Oscar Erickson."

"Ah, " said the doctor. "One of the Scandinavians from Swedetown?"

Libby nodded.

"I certainly do know your uncle."

Libby held her breath. The doctor knew him, but she didn't. She shifted from one foot to the other, waiting to see what trouble they would be in now.

"It's strange that you should be waiting for him, though. I thought I'd heard he left on the train for Detroit. Fed up with the strike and looking to get a job from Mr. Henry Ford. Strange you didn't know he'd gone. And, tell me, why are you carrying a big flag?"

But the doctor never got an answer. To Libby's relief the wooden door was flung open and banged against the wall, setting all the glass jars along the shelves tinkling. A man, gasping and out of breath, plunged through the doorway. "Cyrus! Come! Your brother needs you to get

44

his medical bag and come. There's trouble down by the C&H. It's those strikers again."

Dr. Westerberg gave Libby and Nathan one quick searing look. "You may remain here until I return," he said. He moved purposefully toward a door that connected his office to Dr. Simon Westerberg, MD's office next door. The messenger, still breathing heavily, paid no attention to them as he followed the dentist's long strides.

"See, brothers." Libby reminded Nathan that she had guessed correctly.

"Uncle Oscar? Who's Uncle Oscar? Why did you tell him that?"

"Well, we had to say something, so I used my great - grandfather's name. Anyhow, you weren't being any help."

Nathan only scowled at her. They heard the outside door of the next office bang and their attention was caught by the figures of the dentist and the other man rushing past the window.

"Let's go," Libby said, moving toward the door. Spotting a large wooden cabinet near the door Libby shoved the flag and pole behind it until it was completely hidden. "There must be an emergency, an accident or something. C'mon."

"But, he told us to stay here. And it's cold out there." Nathan's voice rose to a whine. He looked from the warm stove to Libby and back again.

"Stay then, Wimp. I'm going." Just as Libby reached the door she spied a coat rack. A couple of coats hung from wooden pegs. She threw one toward Nathan and scrambled into the other. It surely belonged to the tall dentist. It hung down to Libby's ankles. She pushed the sleeves up. She gave Nathan one last glare and pushed through the door. She smirked when she saw that Nathan followed her. "They went this way," she said.

Turning right when they reached the wooden sidewalk, she yelled, "Run. It will help us stay warm." She began to run toward the corner, trying to keep the tall figure of Dr. Westerberg and his companion in sight. They turned at the next corner and Libby lost sight of them. But once she reached the corner it was not hard to see where they had gone. A few blocks ahead Libby could see a large crowd of people. Even from this corner she could hear the noise. People shouted. Horses neighed. Metal banged.

She stopped to get her breath and let Nathan catch up. He came up beside her, bent over, and clutched his side. "I've got a terrible pain in my side," he panted. "I can't run any more."

Libby looked up the street and then back at Nathan. For the first time she noticed the snow. The wooden sidewalks had been clear. But the streets were hard packed snow. Mounds of dirty brown snow rose down the middle of the street making a sort of boulevard, separating one side from the other. When she looked closer Libby saw the tracks of horse shoes and sled runners in the snow pack. She bit on the skin on the side of her thumb as she considered Nathan. "Pain - drain," she mumbled around the thumb. She really wanted to see what was happening up ahead. She had read enough, in her research, to know that if it really was 1913, it might be a fight between striking miners and deputies or mine managers. Maybe Big Annie was there. She didn't want to miss the chance to see history happening. But she also realized that if she and Nathan became separated in that crowd, they might never find each other. And, unfortunately, they needed each other. She gave the crowd up ahead one last longing look, turned back to Nathan, and sighed, waiting for him to catch his breath.

Chapter 10

"There must be a thousand people here," Libby said, awed by the crowd they approached. "All I can see is the backs of tall people." She leaned left, then right, stood on her tip-toes. "We'll never see what's happening from here. C'mon. Let's sneak up."

Nathan took a step backward. "Uh-uh," he said, shaking his head. "That looks dangerous. I'll just stay back here. You go ahead if you want. I'll meet you right here when you've had enough."

"Promise you won't move?"

"Cross my heart." He made an "x" over his chest.

Libby was torn between wanting to see what was happening ahead and wanting to stay with the only person she knew in this crowd. Eventually her curiosity won. "Okay. You'd better be right on this spot when I come back." As she turned from him she thought she heard him say, "If you come back in one piece." She ignored it.

She began to wiggle under arms and between bodies, edging closer and closer to the front of the crowd. Her face was rubbed red by the rough wool fabrics of jackets as she squeezed past. It took forever but finally she squeezed through the last tiny opening between two long coats and found herself at the front of the crowd that lined the street.

Soldiers on horseback lined up along the street, about as far apart as their arms could reach, facing the crowd. They made a human-horse rope to keep the crowd from surging forward. On the other side of the street about a hundred women and children, along with striking miners carrying signs, chanted and waved banners and signs. A few of the signs, written in English, Libby could read. "One man drill - widow maker" said one. Another read, "Striking for safer work conditions." But many of the signs were written in languages Libby could not read. Some of the women and children banged wooden spoons on pots, making the loud metal noises she had heard.

People in the crowd on Libby's side of the street, mostly men, yelled at the striking miners and their supporters across the street. A man near Libby shouted bad words, words that Libby knew could get a kid in big trouble. One of the soldiers brought his horse close to the curser, so close that Libby could smell the ripe horse smell. He pointed a club at the man and warned, "Sir, watch your language. There are women and children here."

"Bah!" the man shouted back. He spit at the ground in front of him. "That's what I think of those women. Why don't they go home where they belong?" Then he shrank back into the crowd, away from the soldier. A real brave gentleman, Libby thought. Her eyes scanned the protestors across the street, looking for a tall woman. She was sure she could recognize Big Annie from the picture if she was here.

Except for yelling, the crowds on both sides of the street seemed peaceful. Libby wondered what the emergency was that had required Dr. Westerberg, the dentist, to bring Dr. Westerberg, the doctor's, medical bag. Then she saw that down the street a little further, toward the front of the line of strikers, there was a commotion. She sidled her way carefully, trying to move to the right while still staying near the front of the crowd. Finally she got close enough to see. What she saw was a striking miner lying on the wooden sidewalk across the street. Both Dr. Westerbergs bent over him. His face was covered with bright red blood. "What happened to him?" she asked a bearded man next to her, pointing at the bloodied man.

"Caught a rock or a piece of brick, I guess," the man replied. "But up there is where the real trouble is. That Annie Clemenc is causing a fracas again." He pointed a little farther up the street where Libby could see a group of soldiers on horseback in a line advancing toward the group of women. At the front stood a tall woman in a white dress, carrying a large flag on a pole.

Libby's breath caught in her throat. It's her! It's Big Annie! She stood frozen to the spot, watching the action. Annie looked just like her picture. Except that without the half-teeth smile, she did not look pretty, only fierce. It felt to Libby like she was watching a movie she'd seen before. She knew what was happening. A shiver went up her spine. The hairs on the back of her neck felt like they were sticking straight out when she realized that she'd just read about it.

Annie did not stop when the soldiers approached her. She walked head on into the troops carrying her flag high. A soldier on horseback drew out his sword and swung it toward Annie. The whole crowd sucked in its breath. Libby could hear a loud whooshing "Ohhhhhhhh" sound from all around her. A woman across the street screamed.

The sword hit Annie's flag pole and knocked the flag from her hands. It fell into the snow and mud at her feet.

One of the men marchers stepped forward and bent to help her pick up the flag. Another soldier pushed him to the ground. A third soldier slashed at the flag with his sword, ripping a long gash in the red and white silk. The hooves of his horse stomped the flag into the mud. A moan rose up from the crowd.

But still Annie did not give up. She dropped to her knees in the mud, her fingers grabbing at the tattered flag. She lifted it, dripping mud, and hugged it tightly to her chest. Deputies and soldiers surrounded her, tugging at the edges of the flag, trying to wrest it from her grip.

But Annie held fast. She stood up then, tall and proud, mud splattering the front of her white dress. "Kill me!" she shouted, her eyes sending sparks. "Run your bayonets and sabers through this flag and kill me, but I won't move. If this flag will not protect me, then I will die with it!"

The three soldiers took a menacing step closer, each with his sword held tight, pointing toward Annie's chest. Annie stood firm, clutching the flag, staring defiantly at them. From behind her movement began. The strikers and their backers seemed to flow like water around Annie, surrounding her. They separated her from the soldiers and she seemed to disappear right before Libby's eyes.

Libby realized she'd been holding her breath. She let it out in a long whoosh. That was the bravest thing she had ever seen. When she had read about it, it had seemed exciting. But now, witnessing the event, she could appreciate the danger and courage that were part of Annie Clemenc's life.

Just when she'd found her, Annie had disappeared, melted into the crowd. Libby strained, trying to see a tall woman among the people across the street. But she was nowhere in sight. She had disappeared, probably for her own safety, so she wouldn't be hurt, or arrested again, so she could return to march another day and another.

Libby drifted back through the crowd to where she had left Nathan. She knew she hadn't seen the last of Big Annie. She knew where she could find her, and when. Early tomorrow morning Annie would be leading the marchers again, carrying a flag on a ten foot pole, the rallying symbol of the striking miners.

Early tomorrow morning. Libby stopped walking so suddenly that a man coming up behind her bumped into her, almost toppling her over. He reached out a steadying arm. "Sorry, little missy," he apologized and hurried on. Tomorrow morning she would have to be on this street watching for Big Annie. But where would she spend the night? How could she and Nathan manage in this strange and cold place where they knew no one and didn't even have their jackets?

Chapter 11

"Libby! Over here!" Nathan waved to her from the street corner right where she had left him. "What took you so long?"

"It was Big Annie. I saw her. She was so brave. You should have seen her, Nathan. The soldiers were coming at her, on their horses, their swords pointing right at her. One of them went Slash!" Libby acted out the scene, slashing her arm through the air in front of Nathan. "He slammed her flagpole to the ground. Another soldier went R-r-r-rip! And cut the flag to shreds. Annie wasn't scared. She picked it up, all muddy, and held onto it and said she'd die with it if she had to. Oh, she was totally awesome." Libby's eyes shone as she recalled Annie holding the tattered flag, standing up for what she believed in.

"Yeah. Whatever." Nathan shrugged, still hugging himself tightly for warmth. "I almost froze to death waiting for you. I don't think this is even a winter jacket."

Libby made a frog face at him. "I bet if you got the chance to see Benedict Arnold in person, in action, you wouldn't say 'whatever'."

"I would if I was freezing to death," he insisted. "Now that you have seen your hero, can we go someplace warm and talk about how we're going to get out of here? I want to go home!"

Libby didn't even want to think about that right now. She'd worry about that later. Right now her brain was filled with thoughts of Big Annie. A gifted and talented person would not just give up and go home. She was sure of that. A gifted and talented person would take advantage of the opportunity she'd somehow, mysteriously and magically been given. A gifted and talented person would try to get to know Big Annie and everything about her so she could do a really gifted and talented job in History Alive! Ms. Sullivan expected it of her. And, she discovered, she expected it of herself.

"First we'd better return these jackets before the dentist has us arrested for stealing," Nathan said as they walked back down the wooden sidewalk. The long arms of his jacket flapped at his sides. Libby put each of her hands up into the opposite sleeves, clutched her arms in front of her and used the sleeves as a muff to keep her hands and arms warm. Pressing them against her chest helped warm her middle. The long coat flaps helped warm her legs, and the prospect of meeting Big Annie warmed her thoughts.

*   *   *   *

Dr. Cyrus Westerberg, DDS, had not returned yet, so Libby and Nathan put the coats back on their hooks and made a bee-line toward the warmth of the black wood stove. They stood close and held their hands out to the radiating heat.

"Look at this antique dentist's chair," Libby said, pointing to the black metal chair with silver trim, a thin leather seat, and head rests that looked like ear muffs.

Nathan didn't even look up. "What are we gonna do, Libby? The doctor will be back soon with all his questions and his eagle eyes."

"How should I know?" Libby grumped.

"Well, you're the one who got us into this mess. Now you can just figure out how to get us out of it."

"Me? You're the one who tried to grab my flag and pushed me into the mirror. You caused it all."

"Did not."

"Did too." Libby crossed her arms and looked out from under her eyebrows, making her stubborn mule face at him.

Nathan dropped his gaze first. He walked away from the stove, toward the back of the dentist's office where he disappeared into the dark. Libby pretended not to notice. She wished he'd just disappear for good. But when he didn't come back after several minutes she began to wonder where he was, what he was doing. She stomped down on her curiosity, stayed stubbornly by the stove, and waited for the warmth to get through to her bones.

"Hey, Libby. There's a bed back here, a skinny little one. I wonder why a dentist would have a bed."

Libby gave up her anger and went to see. The small dim backroom contained only a wooden stool and the narrow cot with a thin pillow at one end and a blanket folded at the other. "Maybe it's for emergencies," Libby guessed. "Maybe sometimes he gives his patients too much anesthesia and they have to lay down for a while. Probably they get so dizzy and their mouths hurt and they can't walk." Libby swayed around the tiny room, spinning and bumping into the wall and the door pretending to be so dizzy she couldn't walk. "Dizzy-whizzy. Pain-complain," she chanted. She moaned and held her jaw. "Oh-h-h-h." She threw herself onto the cot, pretending to faint. Then she giggled.

Nathan apparently didn't think she was a gifted and talented actress. "Quit goofing around and start thinking," he ordered. "If the dentist has a cot, the other one-the doctor- must have at least one, maybe two for his patients. If we can't figure out how to get home, maybe we could hide and stay there for the night."

Libby jumped up. "Nathan, you are finally using your big fat brain. Let's go." She headed for the door that connected the two offices. Nathan smoothed out the sheet and pillow on the cot before he followed.

"You were right. Look. There are two examining rooms and there's a small, hard bed in each."

Nathan nodded with an I-told-you-so smirk. "We'd better be quiet so we can hear if they come back." No sooner had those words come out of his mouth than they heard the outside door slam and two male voices talking.

Chapter 12

Carefully and quietly Nathan and Libby crept behind the door of the small examining room and strained to hear. Mostly they heard the low rumble of the two male voices. But then suddenly the voices grew louder. They could hear footsteps coming closer to where they hid. Libby sucked in her breath and held it. She felt Nathan shiver beside her. The doctors were very close. Were they coming into this room? Libby brought her left hand up to her mouth and bit down on her knuckles. The footsteps stopped, but not the voices.

"Don't know where those two strange children went. I told them to stay put." That was the dentist.

"Probably got warm and then ran off home." That was the doctor.

"I don't know. There was something strange about them, but I didn't get the chance to find out what. Joe came running, ordering me to fetch your medical bag."

"Yes. Blast it. Haven't we had enough blood shed over this strike? I never thought it would last this long – five months. Maybe now that we've formed the Citizens' Alliance against the strike, the miners will give up. Surely they'll know it's a lost cause. Then the violence and bloodshed can finally stop," said the doctor.

"I wouldn't be so sure. The Alliance might help,

especially if the storekeepers refuse to give any more credit to the strikers. But if that Annie Clemenc keeps stirring them up, well, I just don't know, " said the dentist.

"One thing I know for sure is that it's past time for lunch and I'm hungry. Let's go."

Both sets of footsteps moved away and soon the outer door banged shut. "Whew," Libby said. "I guess we're safe for now."

"Speaking of hungry," Nathan said, "I'm starving. What are we going to do for food?"

Libby looked around the bare, dim room. "It's for sure we won't find anything to eat here. We'll have to leave before they come back anyhow. But we have to figure out how to get back in later."

Without a word she and Nathan began to search the offices. There was a back door, but it had a heavy iron latch on the inside. No good. In the other examining room they found a small window above the bed. Nathan climbed onto the bed, unlatched the metal window lock and pushed up on the window frame. Luckily it creaked open. "If we leave this unlocked I think we'll be able to crawl in and out," he announced.

Nathan began to hoist himself up to the opening.

"Wait." Libby ran back through the doctor's office and the dentist's office, grabbed the jackets off their hooks, and returned to where Nathan waited half in and half out of the window. "Here. Toss these out first. They'll keep us warm and be soft to land on."

Nathan scrambled through the opening. Libby heard a thump outside as he landed. "Ow!" he yelped. "It's a bigger drop than I thought. I'll help catch you, Libby."

Libby tried to climb up to the window but her long dress made it practically impossible. "Dress – stress," she grumbled. On the third try she gathered up the skirt in front and tucked the bunched up fabric into her underwear, hoping Nathan wouldn't notice. She thought again about how difficult it was for girls to wear long dresses all the time in the old days. But on that third try she made it. She dropped down on top of Nathan and they landed in a jumble on the snow.

"We've got to quit doing this," Nathan said, rubbing a sore elbow as he got up.

They shrugged into their big jackets. As Libby buttoned hers she mumbled, "I hope Dr. Westerberg doesn't notice these are missing."

"Yeah. That's all we'd need is the police after us. That would be the last straw." Nathan looked up the alley way in one direction, and then in the other. "Which way?"

Libby shrugged. "Eenie-meanie-miney-mo." She pointed. "Catch a tiger by the toe." Her finger pointed to the left and they followed it.

Chapter 13

At the end of the alley they made another turn, at the corner another. Libby tried to remember, left, right, left so they could find their way back later. They could see nothing that looked like it would have food. There were stores, mostly hardware and equipment. And bars. There were several bars. But no restaurants, no mini-mart convenience stores.

"I'd give anything for a McDonalds or a Taco Bell," Nathan said.

"First, they didn't have fast food in 1913," Libby informed him, happy to be able to tell Nathan the facts. "Second, we don't have any money."

"Oh yeah? Maybe you don't. But I've got four quarters. It was P.T.A.'s popcorn day at school and I was going to buy a bag for myself and some for my friends." Nathan dug the quarters out of his pocket.

"We're saved!" Libby said. "I bet you can buy all sorts of food with a dollar back in the olden days. The miners only earned $2.50 a day." She stopped and looked shrewdly at Nathan. "You are going to share, aren't you?"

Nathan put the quarters back in his pocket. "Maybe," he said. "But first we've got to find a store."

They walked on, searching each sign and store window. Finally at a corner Libby looked up the street and saw what they'd been searching for. A large, two story brick building rose up. On the first floor there were two businesses, a pool hall–tavern and an A&P grocery store.

"Let's go," she commanded as she dashed into the street.

"Libby! Watch Out!" Nathan screamed. Libby stopped in her tracks and jumped back just in time as an old-fashioned streetcar lumbered past.

"Geez, Libby, That was close. You better be more careful."

"Careful – swearful," Libby replied. She tried to sound casual but inside her heart was pounding. It had been a close call. But she was so hungry and so anxious to get to the A&P store that she hadn't looked both ways before dashing into the street. She shook her head. She hadn't done anything that stupid since she was two years old.

Before stepping into the street again she made sure to check both ways. Who knew there would be trolleys or streetcars or whatever it was that had nearly run her over? Safely across the street, she and Nathan headed directly for the grocery store. As they got closer they could read the signs. "The Great Atlantic & Pacific Tea Co." it said over the store. One word hung over the entrance to the pool hall – tavern. "Vairo," it said. Libby hadn't a clue what that meant. Maybe it was the owner's name, she thought. Nathan tipped his head back and read the sign high on the second story of the building. "Societa Mutua Beneficenza Italiana." It sounded to Libby like it might be "Society to benefit Italians."

"Hmmmmmmmmm. Big Annie had something to do with an Italian hall. I'm just getting to that in my research." Libby thought for a moment. "Now I remember. She was planning a Christmas party there for the children of the striking copper miners. The party was going to be at The Italian Hall on the afternoon of Christmas Eve. But then I had to stop reading because it was time for gym class. So I don't know if it was a good party or not."

"I just hope we're not still here at Christmas to find out," Nathan said sourly. Libby hadn't thought about that. She'd never been away from home for Christmas. It would be very weird not to be with her family. But still.......

"Well, maybe.........."

"No, Libby. Absolutely not. Don't even think about it. We are getting out of here and going home as soon as possible. Now let's get some food."

As they entered the A&P store a bell jangled over the door. It did not look like any grocery store Libby had ever been in. It certainly wasn't like the huge Econo-Valu where her Mom shopped. It seemed dark without the fluorescent lights she was used to. From just inside the door Libby and Nathan surveyed the store. It was long and deep and lined with rows of tall wooden shelves. There were bins of loose potatoes and onions, barrels of pickles, shelves of canned and packaged foods. Across the back of the store stood a big white enameled meat cooler with a glass front.

To their right a stout lady in a big white apron guarded a glass counter with an old fashioned cash register. To their left a magazine and newspaper rack stood. Libby moved toward the newspapers, trying to read the headlines and counting aloud. "Nathan, look. There are nine newspapers in Calumet and only one of them is in English."

"Whatever," Nathan replied. "We're looking for food, not reading material," he reminded her.

Libby followed him down a narrow isle. Their heads swiveled, eyes scanning the shelves. She couldn't find any of her favorite snacks. No nacho chips. No Twinkies or Oreos. Not even any apples. "Here's bread," she said, grabbing up a small loaf in a white paper bag and showing it half-heartedly to Nathan.

"Look at this, Libby." Nathan held out a jar and Libby read the label. "Nut Meal."

"I think it must be like peanut butter. But it says the peanuts are boiled," Nathan reported.

"That doesn't sound as good as honey roasted, super chunk, does it? Boiled peanuts? Yuck."

"Have you ever thought that you might have arachibutyrophobia?"

Libby gave him a puzzled look. "What's that?"

"The fear of peanut butter sticking to the roof of your mouth." He smirked at her.

Leave it Nathan to know something like that. "We'll buy it. We can make sandwiches. Look. Here's jam." Libby held up a jar. "Mrs. O'Mally's Strawberry Preserves. All right! PB&J sandwiches. My favorite."

"I hope we've got enough money," Nathan said as they headed for the cash register.

They had more than enough. Enough, in fact, to add two big dill pickles wrapped in waxed paper, and a pile of penny candy.

"Imagine. Penny candy. Even two-for-a-penny candy. That's one good thing about being in the past," Libby said. She watched Nathan stick a long black licorice into his mouth. "Your mouth is going to turn black," she informed him. She stuck a red sucker into her mouth. If she swiveled it over her lips a lot she bet it would look like she was wearing lipstick.

They stepped out of the store as the bell jangled again

over their heads. Outside in the cold Nathan flapped the long sleeves of his jacket. "Now what? Have you thought about how to get back home, back to our own time yet?"

Libby looked at him with impatience. "No, Nathan. I'm working on it. Just quit nagging at me. Think for yourself. You're supposed to have such a big, smart, gifted and talented brain. Use it for a change." She stomped away. After several steps she turned around to see if Nathan was following but he stood still in the same spot in front of the A&P door. She turned back.

"If you want to think about getting home, all I can tell you is that last time when this happened, I got home by doing the exact same things. You do whatever you want. I'm going to try to find Big Annie before I think about going home." She turned again and walked purposefully away. Nathan did not follow. Libby didn't care. She was tired of his complaining and whining. She wanted a little adventure while she was here in Calumet.

She walked on and on, peering into store windows, looking into the faces of every person she passed, watching for a tall lady with brown hair pulled back into a knot and a half smile on her mouth. On and on she searched but Annie was not to be found. She's probably at home cooking supper or at the church taking care of crippled miners, Libby thought. I'll never find her this way. I'll just have to wait until morning and go to the street where they parade.

That decided, Libby thought maybe she should start back toward Dr. Westerberg's office She was getting very cold, especially her feet. As she thought about the food Nathan had, she realized she was also very hungry. It must be supper time.

She stood on a corner looking up at the street signs. "Signs – mines – whines," I should have paid attention to the street names." She wasn't sure she knew how to find the doctors' offices. "I'm pretty sure it's this way," she said confidently and headed down a wide street. This time she kept a watchful eye for streetcars. But the shops she saw did not look familiar. She'd better head in another direction. She did a U-turn and headed off, a little less confidently. But again nothing looked familiar.

As she turned down another street she realized that the sun no longer shone, that the streets and shops were looking darker, grayer. "Oh, no. It's getting dark. I've got to find my way back soon," she said.

She tried to push the panic down before it could rise up and take over her brain. But as it quickly got darker the panic monster crept higher within her until it rose to her throat, making a raw thick lump that she could hardly breathe around.

Take a deep breath, Libby, she reminded herself. A gifted and talented person wouldn't panic. She would think of a way. Okay. What would a gifted and talented person do right now? Probably she wouldn't go running off in any old direction without knowing where she was or where she was going. Suddenly it came to her and she knew what she should do. She should ask for directions. She looked up the darkening street and saw two men coming out of a tavern.

She took a deep breath and walked up to them. "Excuse me," she said loudly. "Can you tell me which way to go to get to Dr. Westerberg's office?"

The men looked at her and then at each other. Each man said something to the other, but Libby couldn't understand any of it. It was a strange, guttural sounding language. One of the men looked again at her, raised a hand on each side of his shoulders and said, "No English."

"Oh," said Libby. She tried to swallow past the lump growing in her throat. She walked past them hoping she could find someone else to ask, someone who spoke English.

A dirty looking old man with a tangled gray beard, wearing a long grubby coat and red knitted cap approached her. He looked a little scary. Suddenly she remembered her mother's warnings about not talking to strangers, and this grubby old man certainly looked strange. But it was getting dark and Libby was getting desperate. She tried again.

"Certainly." He pointed to his left. "Take a left turn at the next corner. Then continue East. Just follow that old copper moon." He touched his hand to his hat in a salute.

"Thank you," Libby said gratefully, glad that he had turned out to be a gentleman. She turned the corner the old man had said, and there she saw a big round moon hanging just over the tops of the buildings on that street. Glowing soft and golden, it looked like a copper disk suspended in a deep navy blue sky. The moon gave a surprising amount of golden light to the street. It pushed back the dark shadows and the lump of panic.

She started walking toward it. A big, round, full moon, she thought. A copper-colored disk lighting her way. Libby smiled and headed more confidently toward the copper moon, Dr. Westerberg's office, and Nathan.

Chapter 14

"Where in the heck have you been?" Nathan asked as Libby rushed through the door in a blast of cold air. She had gone around the back of the doctors' office and thrown a small stone at the window they had crawled through earlier. Nathan's face popped up on the other side of the glass.

"Open up. I'm freezing," she'd said. He had lifted the metal latch on the back door and let her in. "Exploring," she answered. "Why do you have the lights on? Use your head, Nathan. If we put lights on someone will notice and they'll find us. And then what will we do?"

Nathan laughed at her worry. "Nah," he said. "Dr. Westerberg gave me permission to stay here."

"What? How did that happen?"

"Actually he came back and caught me sleeping in here." Libby's eyes widened. Nathan shrugged. "I thought I was a goner for minute, but then I remembered what you told him. So I made up this sad story about how we had come to find your uncle and we got separated and I couldn't find you and this was the only place in Calumet that I knew. And maybe you had found your uncle and forgot all about me. Boo Hoo. So he said I could have a job working for him, running errands and delivering medicines, because his last boy ran off to Detroit. So, I have a job and a place to sleep as long as I need it." He folded his arms and smirked at her. "And what did you accomplish?"

"Nothing," Libby admitted truthfully.

They ate a supper of bread, peanut butter, jelly and dill pickles, with candy for dessert as they sat on the two cots. Nathan wanted to talk about a plan to get home. Libby just wanted to sleep. Her mind drifted. It was funny how she didn't feel really scared or homesick. She wondered if it was because someone from home was here with her sharing the adventure. Even if it was Nathan Westlake. Somehow having him here made it seem not quite so scary and strange as it would have been alone.

Libby's head began to nod. Nathan was still droning on and on about making a plan, but she heard less and less of what he was saying. Finally she fell over on her side on the cot right in the middle of one of Nathan's sentences. "Good night, Nathan," she mumbled as she lifted her legs onto the cot and pulled the thin blanket up to her chin.

"Listen, Libby," Nathan began. But he realized she was already deeply asleep.

*   *   *   *   *   *

In the morning Nathan was first to wake. He'd set his watch alarm for 6:30 and it was still dark when it began to beep. "Wake up, Libby," he said, shaking her shoulder. "You've got to be out of here by the time the doctor comes."

Libby sat up quickly, instantly and completely awake. "Thank goodness it's still dark," she said. "I've got to get over to Eighth and Elm street where we saw Big Annie yesterday. She'll be marching at daybreak." Libby tired to smooth out the wrinkles in her dress, thinking, Gee, I look like I slept in it, which, of course, she had.

"Doesn't Big Annie ever take a day off?" Nathan asked.

"Nope. Never. She's been marching for five months, every single morning. I bet she's marched about a thousand miles by now! And, listen to this, Nathan. She's been arrested three times and she spent ten days in jail."

"Sounds dumb to me."

"You don't understand, Nathan. She believes that supporting the strike is the only thing women can do to try to make life better for their families."

"Whatever."

Libby was so sick of Nathan and his 'whatevers'. If he didn't stop saying that about everything she thought was important, one of these days she was going to punch him in the eye and say 'whatever' when he started to cry.

Libby blessed Dr. Westerberg for having indoor plumbing. She tried, not very successfully, to brush her teeth with her finger and a stream of cold water. Pushing her fingers through the tangles, she tried to smooth her hair. She took the doctor's jacket and a piece of bread with jam. "I'll be back after I've met Big Annie," she said as she grabbed the door latch.

"Libby, wait. There's something I found out from the doctor yesterday. You won't believe what day it is. " Nathan paused.

Libby's hand stilled on the latch. "What do you mean? What day is it? Is this important, Nathan? I've got to go."

"Christmas Eve, Libby. The day before Christmas, December 24, 1913."

"No kidding? Wow! That is so cool. I know from my

research that Annie was organizing a party for the children of the striking miners on Christmas Eve. I can go to the party! Oh, that will be so cool-rule. I'll see you when I get back."

"Maybe you'll see me at the party," he called after her. "I have to deliver some stuff there for the doctor. He's donating candy and some other stuff but he doesn't want anyone to know. So I'm delivering it."

"Yeah, whatever," Libby said with a great deal of satisfaction. She swept out the door and followed the same route she and Nathan had taken yesterday, toward the corner of Eighth and Elm Streets and the early morning parade led by Big Annie.

Chapter 15

When she reached the corner of Eighth and Elm Streets Libby looked as far down the snowy road as her eyes could see. Sure enough. There they were – a large group of people marching together toward her, filling the street. In the front of the marchers a tall woman held up a huge flag on a pole. Two streamers hung from the top and a young girl on either side of Annie Clemenc held onto the ends of the streamers.

Libby ran to meet the parade. Her heart pounded fast and hard. She could almost feel her blood fizzing like ginger ale through every vein in her body. Her fingers tingled. The hairs on her scalp seemed to stand up at attention. She didn't even seem to need to breathe. She was the air and the air was her. She felt like she could fly down the street, she was so totally, amazingly thrilled.

And suddenly she was there. She fell into step beside the teenaged girl holding the streamer to Big Annie's right. She matched her footsteps to the girls'. When the girl glanced at her, Libby gave her a friendly smile.

"I'm tired," the girl complained. "My feet hurt. I just want to crawl back into my bed."

"Go ahead,," Libby said. "I'll take your place. Hand me the streamer." The girl did. Libby raised her arm high and looked up to see the white streamer cutting a graceful arc in the lavender morning sky, leading down from Annie

Clemenc's great flag. She smiled her widest Cheshire cat smile and lifted her head proudly. She was here in Calumet, marching down the street with Big Annie, her hero, trying to better the lives of miners and their families. Awesome!

Libby couldn't keep her eyes off Big Annie, just a few feet away to her left. My, she was tall. And pretty, too. Her hair was a glossy brown knot. Her profile dainty with its soft curving cheeks and up-thrust chin. Annie must have felt eyes staring at her because she turned her head and glanced at Libby. Libby's heart nearly melted when Annie flashed her that beautiful half-teeth smile. Libby smiled back widely, with all her teeth. Then she saw a change come to Annie's expression. A puzzled frown replaced the smile, making a furrow down her forehead, between her eyes. She stared at Libby for a long moment. Have I done something wrong? Libby wondered. Then she shrugged it off. Maybe she's just thinking that she doesn't recognize me, Libby decided.

A noisy commotion broke out somewhere behind them in the parade. Libby tore her gaze from Annie and swiveled to see what was happening. The clatter of spoons and pots had increased. The chanting of the children got louder. "Papa is striking for us. Papa is striking for us," reverberated between the buildings.

"Scabs! Scabs!" she heard women shriek. Several of them, carrying brooms, brandished them toward three men who scurried along the sidewalk, carrying lunch buckets, headed toward the mine.

Annie stopped marching and turned to face these men. "You would steal the jobs from our husbands and sons?" she shouted at the replacement workers.

The men put their heads down pretending not to hear or see. They walked faster.

"Attack them, Ladies!" she shouted. The women broke ranks and ran after the men, pounding at them with their brooms. Filth flew from the brooms as they made contact with the heads of the three men. "Ha, ha!" Annie's laugh boomed. "You scabs! Your souls are as filthy as these brooms we've dipped into the outhouses!"

"Oh, yeah, you show 'em, Annie," Libby said aloud. Then she thought about what she'd heard. Outhouses? Oh, yuck. Libby couldn't believe it. Thinking about it was enough to make a person sick. She caught a fleeting glance at the horrified, humiliated face of one of the men as he shook his head. His eyes touched hers in a second of sadness. Then he clasped his lunch bucket to his chest and ran. How awful! Libby couldn't imagine how the women could do such a thing to someone, even if he was on the opposite side in the strike. For a moment she wasn't sure whether she liked Annie Clemenc at all. She felt like a balloon that had been poked with a needle. All the air, all the excited fizz had gone out of her. She stood there in the road feeling little and lost.

Then a finger poked her on the shoulder. She turned to look at the finger poking her. The finger moved across her chest to point toward the pin on the front pleat of her dress.

"Who are you? Where did you get that pin?" Annie Clemenc asked her.

Chapter 16

Should Libby tell her the pin was from her grandpa Erickson in Arizona? Or should she say it was from the made-up uncle here in 1913? Which one would make sense right now? Which one would Annie believe without questioning? Libby was getting all confused in her lies. She knew the best thing was to tell the truth. But right now it was just so complicated. She sighed. "From my uncle," she said finally.

"Your uncle's name?"

"Oscar. Oscar Erickson." Her great-grandfather's name. Oh, the lies were all tangling up together now.

Annie nodded her head slowly. "I thought so," she said, her voice low. There was no smile on Annie's face now. No sparkle lit her eyes. Her shoulders seemed to sag. She lowered her head for a long moment and took a deep breath. When she raised her face and looked at Libby, she seemed thoughtful and sad. Libby stared into her eyes. She recognized those sad eyes. She'd seen them before. She blinked her own eyes twice in confusion, and then looked back into Annie's. Could it be? Could those be the same sad, strange eyes she'd seen in the old mirror? Eyes-surprise-recognize, Libby thought. She pulled her elbows in to her sides and tried to shake herself free of the weird feeling creeping up her back. Think about something else, she told herself.

"Do you know my...uncle?"

"Do I know him? Does a woman know her own heart?"

What a strange way to answer, Libby thought.

Annie touched her finger again to Libby's copper leaf pin. Gently she traced the outline. "Did you know Oscar made that pin?"

Libby shook her head. She knew it had belonged to her great-grandpa, but she didn't know he had made it. "Really?"

"Yes," Annie answered. "Come, We'll end the parade for today. We must talk. Then I have to prepare for the children's Christmas party for this afternoon."

"Could I help you with the party?"

"You do not want to be a guest? Meet Santa Claus? Get a gift? Eat some sweets?" Annie quizzed.

"Well, eat the sweets, maybe," Libby said with a grin that Annie returned. She felt happy that she had made Annie smile again. "But I would rather help you work at the party."

"Yes. You must be Oscar's niece. That is just what he would say, too, I think. Come." She reached for Libby's hand. "We must get some cocoa to warm our bones before we can do any work. I have some in the kitchen at the Italian Hall, where the party will be."

Annie led Libby down the streets. Libby had to practically run to keep up with the woman's long strides. Libby found that she wasn't going to need the cocoa to warm up. Just trying to half-run to keep up with Annie was making her warm enough. Soon they came to the large brick building Libby remembered from yesterday with the pool hall and tavern on one side, the A&P grocery store on the other. Annie led her through an arched doorway on the building's far left, and then up twenty-two steep stairs. At the top of the stairs they turned right and entered a massive hall.

Libby could see folding chairs and tables, a large old-fashioned wooden piano, and a raised stage at the far end. A big throne-like chair sat on the stage. Probably for Santa, she decided. She could smell the piney aroma of three large, but bare, Christmas trees.

She followed Annie across the hollow expanses of the floor. Their footsteps echoed in the huge empty room. They went to the far side of the stage and down a narrow set of steps to the kitchen under the stage. Annie hung her coat and Libby's on hooks on the wall.

"Sit," Annie ordered, pointing to a worn wooden table and two chairs. Libby sat as Annie poured milk from a round glass bottle into a tin pot on the black cook stove. While the milk heated she tied a flowered apron over her dress, put another chunk of wood into the stove, and found two cups. She poured chocolate syrup into the cups and set them on the table, one in front of Libby, one across from her. Libby saw that her ceramic cup had a chip out of the top so she turned it around. Finally the milk was hot enough and Annie poured it slowly into the cups, stirring with a dark metal spoon.

"There now. There is nothing better than hot cocoa on a frosty morn, is there?" she said after she had sat down across from Libby and taken her first sip.

"For sure," Libby agreed.

Annie seemed content to sit quietly, sipping her cocoa. But not Libby. Questions were bubbling up inside her, like a bottle of soda pop when it's been shaken. There was so much she wanted to know and she had no idea how much time or how many opportunities she'd have to talk to Annie. "So, you know my uncle Oscar?" she began.

"Ah, yes. I knew Oscar. Knew him as well as I know myself." She sighed and looked directly into Libby's eyes.

"Did he never speak of me? No, of course not. Not to his family. Just as I never spoke of him to mine after……" her voice trailed off.

"After what?" Libby asked, intrigued

Annie looked at her closely. "Ah, you are probably too young to have known." She stared down into her cocoa as if seeing the past there.

"Known what?" Jeepers, it was hard to get her to finish a story.

"Oscar Erickson was my first love," she finally said, sadly. "We loved each other truly, thinking, as young people do, that no one before had ever loved like us. But our families…. mine Austrian, his Swede. They live in the same town, work in the same mines, but they are from different worlds. In our world there was no place for a Protestant Swede. Different traditions, different languages, but mostly, different religions. And in his Swedish world there was no place for a Catholic girl. She gave a rueful smile. "It could not be. My family had already chosen a suitable man, a Croatian man of the same religion, for me." She paused.

"But if you really loved each other……?" Libby couldn't believe it. If she really loved somebody she wouldn't let her family or anyone else tell her she couldn't.

Annie shrugged. "In the end our love was not strong enough. Or we were not strong enough for the fight." She reached again to touch Libby's pin. "Oscar made that. He gave it to me. I wore it always, pinned over my heart. See, here, what it says on the back. OELAK. Oscar Erickson Loves Annie Klobuchar. But when my family sent him away, they gave it back to him." She made a snorting sound. "No. They did not give. My father threw it at him. And I, I stood in the upstairs window crying, but I did nothing. It is my shame that I wasn't strong enough to stand up to them, to risk all."

Libby nodded. Maybe that regret was part of the reason Annie was so strong now. It was strange to think that if things had turned out differently, if Oscar hadn't gone on, later met and married her grandmother, had children and grandchildren, she, Libby Larson, wouldn't exist.

"So you married Joseph Clemenc, the man your parents chose?"

"Yes."

"Have you been happy with him?"

Annie shrugged. "We are companionable in many things." She smiled. "But not in this strike and my actions. 'You should be at home, taking care of the house and your husband,' he says to me, 'not parading and causing trouble.' He is worried that the mining company will put us out of our house because of my actions. But I must risk it. I have learned that to be still when your heart is calling out, is not acceptable."

Libby thought she understood a little more about the complexities of the reasons for Annie's defiance now.

Annie laughed. "I tell him he worries like an old woman. I am famous in the newspapers, I tell him. They compare me to Joan of Arc. The mining company will not touch me. It would make them look bad in the newspapers all over the country. So, I will continue to fight until victory is won."

"You are like Joan of Arc. You are a hero," Libby said.

Chapter 17

Annie's laugh rumbled in the small kitchen space under the stage. "Pah! I am no saint. Believe me. I am no hero. I've been in jail, too."

"I know. But you were only...."

Annie laughed. "I was only kicking and pounding on the police car and spitting at the sheriff's men. Not very saintly, do you think?"

Libby shook her head slowly.

"I am only doing what I can, what must be done to help the miners. They deserve what they are asking for. Their families deserve it. First, a fair wage of $3.50 for a day's work. Miners in Montana get $4.00 a day. And a shorter work day, not 11-12 hours, then come home too tired to talk to the family or play with the children. And most important, to return to the two man drill. No more 'widow maker'!" She slammed her fist down on the table so hard that the cocoa cups wobbled.

"Widow maker? What's that?"

"The drill, child. It used to be that two men worked a drill together. They watched out for each other. Now the managers said, 'No more two man drill. One man – one drill.' It weighs 150 pounds and the miner holds it up on an iron rod while he drills. If anything goes wrong, if it slips on the rod, if he loses his grip, there is no one there to help. It is too noisy to call out and the next driller might be 500 feet away. The miner dies and his wife is a widow, his children orphans."

"I see," said Libby.

"And speaking of the children, now I must get ready for this Christmas party. The poor children. With their fathers out of work for so many months, it would not be a happy Christmas. So, we make this party for them. Each one will get one present. There will be games and music, dancing and candy sweets. We will make a happy Christmas Eve for them.

Libby was curious about that. "Where did you get the money for the presents and candy and stuff?"

"Some things the women made. Some took apart sweaters and knitted the yarn into mittens and hats. Some made dolls. Men made wooden puzzles and such. Some businessmen donated gifts or sweets. Some people gave money, and the last of the union funds, $57.25, was given for the children. Also, one person, who remains . unknown, gave over a hundred dollars."

"Wow! Who has that much money to give away?" Libby wondered aloud.

Annie's brow creased. "Some say it must be James McNaughton himself who would have so much money."

"Who is James McNaughton?"

"Why, don't you know, child, he is the manager of the Calumet and Heckla Mining company, the C&H, the very mines we're striking against."

"Do you think it was him?"

"That I don't. There may be that much money in that man, but there is not that much kindness. The one who said he would see grass grow over the streets of Calumet before he would recognize the miners' strike? The one who said he would teach us to eat potato peelings? No, I do not think it was him."

"Then who do you think did give the money?"

Annie raised one shoulder. "That I don't know. All I know is that I am grateful for the generosity. Without it, the children's Christmas would be dismal."

"I wish I had some money to give," Libby said. She thought of the four quarters she and Nathan had spent at the grocery store and wished she still had some of them to give to the party. She knew now that you could buy a lot more with a quarter in 1913 than you could in her own time. "But I don't have any money," she admitted sadly.

"You are not alone in that," Annie said. They sat in companionable silence for several minutes, sipping cocoa, while thoughts ran through Libby's mind. Annie didn't have any money either, but she was doing all she could to help the children. She was giving of herself. Suddenly Libby knew that she had something of value that she could give. Not to the children, but to Annie. She put her hands up to the pleats on her chest and slowly unpinned the copper leaf. She put it on her open palm, feeling its warmth there for a moment. Then she held it out toward Annie. "Here, Annie," she said. "I want to give this back to you. It really belongs to you. Merry Christmas."

Annie's eyes glittered with tears as she held the pin in her own palm. She curled her fingers around it and brought her hand up to her heart, keeping it there for a long moment. Then, sadly, she held it out toward Libby. "I cannot take it. It is yours."

"No. Please. It will make me happy to know it is back where it belongs. Besides, it's a Christmas gift. You cannot give back a Christmas gift." She smiled her biggest smile at Annie.

Annie gave her that sweet half-teeth smile she would always remember. "Thank you," She said simply. "I cannot wear it. But I will keep it in my treasure box and I will treasure it always." She held it tightly for another long moment, then slipped it into the deep pocket of her apron.

"Okay," Libby said briskly. "That's enough talk for now. Can I help you get the party ready? I'm a good worker."

"You want to help? Come. I put you to work. " She reached for another apron from the hook on the wall behind her and threw it to Libby. Libby tied it around her waist as Annie said, "You do not want to get your pretty dress dirty. I will go home and change just before the party. But your dress is so pretty."

Also, Libby thought to herself, I don't have anything to change into, or a home to go to! The only place I have here is Dr. Westerberg's back room. And the only person I have is Nathan Westlake. She wondered what Nathan was doing today. How did he think he was supposed to deliver things for the doctor when he didn't know his way around Calumet at all? He's probably lost by now, Libby thought. And if he is, how will I find him?

During the next two hours Annie gave Libby so many jobs to do that Libby began to think she'd be too tired to enjoy the party. She decorated the Christmas trees with balls of cotton fluff, bits of crepe paper, ribbon bows, and tinsel. She spread the tablecloths on the tables and straightened up the chairs. She swept the floor of the huge hall. And she filled up hundreds of little bags full of candy. That's what she was working on when Annie signaled her to take a rest break.

"Here, have a piece of saffron cake," she said, placing a plate with a thick slab of yellow cake stuffed with raisins and nuts on the table in front of Libby. "You did not lie. You are a good worker. Thank you for your help. Rest now before the people begin to arrive. I must run quickly home to change so I can be Santa's helper. I have a red dress to wear." She took off her apron and hung it on a hook on the wall. From another hook she grabbed her brown coat. "I'll be back before you can say 'Jack Rabbit'," she said as she spun out the kitchen doorway.

Libby tried to make her twitchy rabbit face. But she did not have the heart for it. She sat nibbling on the heavy cake and thinking sad thoughts. Mostly she thought about it being Christmas. Was it also Christmas at home? She wondered. What were her mom and little brothers doing? Did they miss her? If it really was the day before Christmas she knew just what they'd be doing. Every level spot in the kitchen would be covered with Christmas cookies and the air would smell so deliciously of the pine tree and the fresh cookies. Her little brothers would be guessing what Santa would bring them that night and stuffing cookies into greedy little mouths. Mom would be reminding them that that wasn't really what Christmas was all about, that it was a celebration of Jesus' birth, and a time for families to be together.

Suddenly an ocean of sadness washed over Libby. She wished she was home, together with her family. Even if it really wasn't Christmas at home, she wished she were there. She bit her bottom lip to stop from crying. "Home-roam-poem" she whispered as she sadly put her head down on her arms on the table.

Chapter 18

"Hey, Beans-for-brains, are you sleeping?"
Libby felt her shoulder being stabbed by a bony finger.
She moaned and peeked up from under her hair. She
knew without looking that it was Nathan. Who else would
call her Beans-for-brains? "What are you doing here?"

"Delivering," he said. "A barrel of chocolate drop
candies for the party. Here, have some." He put a
handful of little brown mounds on the table and sat down
across from her.

Libby lifted her head up. She reached her hand out
and, snapping her pointer finger against the pad of her
thumb, she shot a chocolate drop at Nathan. It bounced
and skidded over the rough table top toward him. He
grabbed it up and popped it into his mouth. "These are
really good."

"Right now I'm sick of candy," Libby said. "I've filled
hundreds of bags full of it. And I sampled while I was
working."

Nathan just nodded as he chomped down on the
another chocolate drop. "I like this old-fashioned candy.
The white stuff inside is sort of like the filling in Oreos."
He chewed and swallowed. "Well, did you get to meet
your hero?"

"Big Annie? I sure did. I've been helping her get
things ready for the Christmas party for the striking

miners' children. It'll be starting soon so she ran home to change. You just missed her. Are you coming to the party? I could introduce you to her."

"Nah, I'm too old for little kids' parties. Besides, I'm not a child of a striking miner. And anyhow, I'm working. I have lots of deliveries to make before Christmas. Listen, Libby, now that you've met Big Annie, can we talk about getting home?"

"Funny. I was just thinking about that," Libby replied. "I was feeling sad about not being home for Christmas."

"Well, don't start crying or acting dumb on me. Anyhow, I don't think it could be Christmas at home. It wasn't Christmas time when we left and we've only been gone for one day."

"Yes, but we don't understand how time works when you travel through it, do we?"

"Well, that's true, I guess," Nathan admitted. "We'll just have to see when we get there. Now, how are we going to get there?"

"I don't know, Nathan," Libby groaned, "and I'm too tired to think."

"You've got to. C'mon, Libby. We've got to figure this out together.

"Whatever." Libby loved using his annoying word on him. It actually made her feel a little more awake, as if it peeled off one layer of tiredness.

Nathan gave her a dirty look. It must be his grizzly bear face, Libby thought.

"I already told you everything I know. I had to do everything all over again, just the same, in the same way, in the same place. Exactly the same. But I don't know if it will work that way again."

"There's only one way to find out. We'll have to try it and see. So, what do we need?"

"Let's see. We still have the same clothes. I hid the flag behind the cabinet in the dentist's office, so we can get that. We need an old mirror on a stand, like the one we fell through in the school storage room. And..... and I need my copper leaf pin." Her glance slid over to the wall where Annie's apron hung on a hook. Was it still in the apron pocket or had Annie taken it home already to put into her treasure box? Oh, no, would Annie have to lose the pin again in order for she and Nathan to get back home, back to their own time? Would she have to steal it from Annie, or should she tell her the truth? She hated how confusing her life was.

"Okay, here's what we'll do," Nathan continued confidently, as if everything were all set. "I'll look for an old mirror at the doctors' and on my deliveries. We'll get your flag and go out to the exact boards on the wooden sidewalk and do the same stuff, have the fight and all, and ZAP! We'll wake up back in our own time."

Libby knew it wasn't going to be quite that easy. "What if you can't find a mirror? What if I can't get the pin back? What......?"

Nathan squinted his eyes. "What do you mean, 'get the pin back'? Back from where? What did you do with it? You didn't lose it, did you?"

"No, I didn't lose it."

"Well, where is it, then?"

Libby swallowed. "I gave it to Big Annie as a Christmas present."

"You what? How could you do such a stupid thing when you knew we had to have everything the same to get back home?"

Libby lowered her gaze. All she remembered is that it had felt so right to give Annie the pin. And she remembered how it had wiped the sadness out of her eyes. "You wouldn't understand," she mumbled.

"Darned right, I don't understand. How could you?" Nathan had sprung from his chair and started pacing along the side of the table, drumming his fingers on its worn surface. Libby just let her head droop. Finally he stopped and let out a big breath. "Well, you'll just have to get it back, that's all."

"I know. I will."

Noises began to filter down into the under-stage kitchen. They could hear the sounds of many heavy winter boots clomping up the stairs to the Italian Hall, the high voices of excited children, and the lower murmurs of their parents.

"Here come the people. I guess the party is about to start. I hope Annie is back."

"You better hope you get that pin back." Nathan headed toward the back of the kitchen and stopped at the window. "I'm not going to try to get down the stairs through that crowd coming up. I'll try the fire escape." He pushed the window up and climbed through. "Yikes! It's just a rickety ladder kind of thing. And it's a long way down." He tested the strength of the first couple of rungs. "I wonder when the fire marshal last inspected it."

Libby went to the window and looked down. "It doesn't look safe, Nathan. If you break your neck, you'll never get back home."

Nathan laughed. "I'm not scared," he said as he scrambled down the ladder. "I'll come back later, after I've found the mirror."

"Good luck," Libby called after him, not believing he'd be lucky enough to find one soon.

Chapter 19

It was a great party! "Golly," Libby said, surveying the crowded hall, "there must be four hundred people here."

A Croatian band had played earlier and there was much dancing and twirling and laughing. People sitting at tables ate cakes and drank lemonade. Annie had introduced Mrs. Theresa Sizer who played the piano so forcefully that the cherries on her hat threatened to bounce right off. Many of the children stepped forward to sing. They sang the same Christmas carols four times in four different languages. Libby could only understand them in English, but she could see that various groups of children sang each song, and she could hear that they all sounded different and yet the same.

Grown-ups stood in groups talking, while keeping watchful eyes on their children. It was loud and it was happy and it was hot.

And now, the moment the children had been awaiting arrived. Annie stood up on the stage near the big throne-like chair. She gave a signal to Mrs. Sizer who stopped playing the piano. Annie put two fingers into her mouth and blew a loud, shrill whistle. She caught Libby's eye, where she stood at the side of the steps leading up to the stage, and winked. Then she whistled again. The crowd quieted. "Whistle – missile," Libby said, deciding she'd ask Annie, later, to teach her how to whistle like that.

"Children," Annie called out in a voice that carried to the farthest corners of the hall. "Soon Santa Claus will be here. " She waited, smiling, while some of the children shrieked and clapped. They pressed closer to the stage, wanting to catch the first glimpse of Santa. Soon the children were twenty deep along the front of the stage. "We must not crowd Santa," Annie said. "Each of you will get the chance to say hello to Santa and I know he has a Christmas gift for each of you. But, we must do this in an orderly way. When Santa comes we will line up, single file, at the steps on this side of the stage." She pointed to her left. "You will go, one at a time, to see Santa, and then you will walk across the stage to the steps on this side." She pointed to her right. "You will walk down those steps to join your parents. Does everyone understand?"

"Yes!" "Ya!" came the loud chorus of responses. Annie put her hand up to cup her ear. "Shhhhhh! Listen. What's that? What do I hear?" She repeated it. The children quieted to listen. It was bells. Jingling bells! Santa's bells!

"Ho, ho, ho," they heard from a deep jolly voice. And then a huge man in a red suit and white fur came onto the stage. The children cheered and jumped and clapped for joy, pressing even closer. But several ladies herded them into line at the stage steps and let just one lucky child at a time climb the steps to Santa and a Christmas gift and a small sack of candy that Libby had filled earlier.

"Libby." She turned her stare from the children and Santa to find Annie approaching. "There are so many children! I am worried that we haven't filled enough bags of candy. Would you go to the kitchen and fill some more? Please?"

"Sure," Libby said.

"You are a God-send," Annie said, smiling her sweetest

half-teeth smile at Libby. Libby glowed. She didn't know, she thought as she turned toward the steps leading down to the kitchen under the stage, if it was God who sent her to the past. But at this moment she was glad to be here at this wonderful party, helping Big Annie.

She had filled two dozen sacks with candy when she heard something strange and scary. A loud voice, carrying over the tops of the children's voices, shouted a single word. "Fire!"

Libby lifted her head and listened. Again the voice yelled "Fire! Fire!" There was a long moment of stunning silence. And then pandemonium. At first Libby sat still at the table listening. Horrible sounds came down to her. Frightened screams. Pounding feet. Parents calling the names of children. "Fire!" she heard yelled over and over. And "Watra!" which might have been fire in another language, or might have been a call for water. Libby didn't know. Could there really be a fire in the hall?

She jumped up from her chair and ran up the few steps into the hall. She looked up first, but saw no flames or smoke. But the people, oh, my gosh, the people were in a panic. They screamed. They pushed. They shoved toward the doorway and the twenty-two stairs leading down from the hall. Parents shouted frantically for children. Arms and hands reached out, trying to claw their way through the mass of humanity at the door, shoving and pushing to get to the stairs. And then what would happen, Libby wondered. What would happen when this stampede, this surging human tidal wave reached the stairs? She did not go in that direction.

"No!" Annie screamed. "Be calm. There is no smoke. There is no fire. Stay where you are!"

Mrs. Sizer sat at the piano and began to play slowly and sweetly. "Silent Night," she played, hoping to calm the panic. But the night was anything but silent. The horrible sounds pounded at Libby until she wanted to cover her ears to block it all out. But still she saw no sign of fire. Could it be somewhere below them in the pool hall or the A&P store, trapping them up here? She felt panic fill her. Her heart hammered in her chest and she had a hard time breathing as she ran back down the five steps to the kitchen, remembering Nathan going out the window and climbing down the rickety ladder. And there he was, Nathan himself, shoving bags of candy into his pockets.

"There's no fire, Libby. I'm pretty sure. I just came from down stairs and everything's okay there. Did you see any sign of fire in the hall?"

Libby shook her head from side to side while she tried to get control of her breathing. Finally she blurted out one word, "No."

"I think it's a hoax. A nasty trick someone played."

"Why would anyone do that?"

Nathan shrugged. "Libby," he grabbed her by the shoulders and shook her. "Libby, listen, I found a mirror. Mrs. Paavoneimi, she runs a dress and hat shop just a few doors away from the doctors' office, she has stomach problems and I had to deliver her some medicine and in her shop she has a mirror on a stand, just what we need. Did you get your pin?"

"You found a mirror?" Libby repeated, dazed. She was having a hard time concentrating on what Nathan was saying.

"Yes. I just told you. Now, what about the pin? Have you got it?"

Libby shook her head. Nathan gave her a disgusted look and made a rude noise.

"I'll get it. Just give me a minute. You go first down the fire escape. I'll get the pin, say good-by to Annie, and then I'll climb down. If we get separated, I'll meet you back at Dr. Westerberg's"

Nathan stood, undecided about leaving her. "Are you sure you'll be okay? You don't look too good."

"Go," she said, and pushed him toward the window. He reached out for another handful of chocolate drops and shoved it in his mouth. He can make a chipmunk face, Libby thought.

She watched Nathan disappear through the window and then turned toward the steps leading into the hall. The noise was different now. The teeming screams and pounding rhythms of panic had ceased. What she heard now were the desolate sounds of shock and grief, heartbroken crying, and muffled, far away shouts for help coming from the stairway. Slowly she ascended the five steps into the hall, not sure what she would see.

The hall no longer teemed with people. Those who remained seemed to be frozen in shock, standing or sitting still as statues, glazed expressions on their faces, not talking, numb. Tables and chairs were knocked over, lying helter-skelter across the floor with the remains of wrapping papers and the smears of trampled cake and candy. One of the Christmas trees had toppled and tinsel lay soggy in puddles of lemonade. The people remained still as a painting, faces blank, eyes wide, staring into nothing.

Libby's eyes searched the dismal room for Annie. There she was, sitting on a folding chair near the stage, holding a small child dressed in a sailor suit in her lap. Her hand brushed brown curls off a smooth, still face. The child did not move. Something about the way his arms hung down limply sent a shiver of foreboding up Libby's spine. She felt the contents of her stomach, all those chocolate drops, rising into her throat. The little boy looked like a rag doll, a dead rag doll.

Libby raised her eyes. She couldn't stand to look at the rag doll any longer. She looked instead at Annie, willed herself not to let her eyes move down to what Annie held in her arms. Look only at Annie. Look only at Annie, she told herself.

Annie, sensing her gaze, raised her head and met Libby's eyes. Tears streamed down her cheeks. "How could this happen? I can't believe this could happen. They're dead, Libby. Lots of them. In the stairway. Crushed. Oh, the children, the poor, poor children." She rocked back and forth. Libby stood frozen. "All I wanted was to make a good party. Make the Christmas happy for the children. But look what tragedy has happened instead." She buried her face in the brown curls of the little boy who still had not moved.

Libby stood there for a long moment, feeling Annie's sorrow reaching into her like tentacles squeezing her heart. She spun around and ran back to the kitchen. If she kept running, death and grief couldn't catch her. She ran to the hooks on the far wall where her jacket and Annie's apron hung. She shrugged into the jacket and reached into the big apron pocket. Her fingers closed around the copper leaf pin. She pulled it out and glanced quickly at it. She couldn't hold it and climb down the ladder. If she put it in her jacket pocket it might fall out and be lost. She'd better pin it onto her dress. With fumbling fingers she finally worked the clasp. She felt the warmth of the pin spreading through her chest. She put her hands on the windowsill and started to climb through, but first she stopped for a moment and looked toward the steps and the hall. "I'm sorry," she whispered. "I'm so sorry, Annie." Then she climbed through the window and made her way down the ladder.

Chapter 20

Libby's feet hit the ground. She had never been so glad to have solid earth under her feet. All the way down the ladder she had been sure that at any moment the rungs would give way, or the whole thing would pull away from the building and collapse. She was beginning to think fate had in mind that she be one of the catastrophes of this horrible day. So when she put both feet on the ground, she was so relieved she could have cried.

She leaned over, hands on her bent knees, gasping in the cold air. The sounds of fire alarms and bells and shouting reached her when the blood quit pounding so loudly in her ears. When she'd gotten her breathing under control she stood up and looked around. There were hundreds of people standing in the street, staring at the Italian Hall. The air was full of voices. The voices grew louder; the crowds pressed in. Libby could not see through the people or over them. And she wasn't sure she wanted to. Not after what Annie had told her, and after seeing the dead child in her arms. She began to push her way through the crowd, listening for people who were speaking English. Everyone was talking. Everyone, it seemed, had an opinion or claimed to have seen something involving the tragedy at the hall.

"It was a man with a white button from The Citizens' Alliance that called fire."

"It was a tall man with a gray beard and a hat pulled over his eyes."

"He had red hair. I think he's a boss at the Red Jacket Mine."

"The sheriff barred the door so the people couldn't get out. Then they trampled each other trying to get to the bottom of the stairs and get out of there."

"It was a short man with a red hunting jacket. My sister saw him with her own eyes."

"He ought to be hung."

"If I catch him, I'll kill him, just like he killed those children."

"When the firemen opened the doors, the people were piled in the stairs like cord wood."

"Like a human avalanche."

Rumors flew through the crowd. Each group of people Libby passed had a story, an eye witness report, a theory about who was responsible.

"It was one of those Waddell men that McNaughton brought in, one of those thugs from New York, here to break the strike."

"It was the Citizens' Alliance. He wore their white button."

"It was a young boy. I saw him scrambling down the ladder and his hair was on fire."

A boy with his hair on fire? Or a boy with fiery red hair? Oh, my gosh, Libby thought.

"He's the new boy, making deliveries for Doc Westerberg. He delivered some medicine to my mother this morning."

It was Nathan they'd seen, climbing down the ladder with his bright red hair. And they're talking about blame and killing. I think we'd better get out of here in a hurry, Libby decided.

She began to run, pushing her way past people without apology. She ran all the way to the green and gold building where the doctor and dentist had their offices. The streets and sidewalks were empty. Everyone, it seemed, was at the Italian Hall, the scene of the disaster. That's a good thing, Libby thought. It will make it easier for us to try to get back to the future.

Banging through the doctor's office door, Libby began yelling for Nathan. "Nathan! C'mon. Hurry! We've got to get out of here fast!"

Nathan wandered in from the back room. He wiped his hands slowly on one of the doctor's white linen towels. "What's your big hurry all of a sudden?"

"We've got to get you out of here. There's a mob at the Italian Hall, looking for someone to blame and punish. Somebody saw you coming down the ladder and said your hair was on fire. Some of them think you are to blame for the disaster. Let's get out of here as fast as we can."

Nathan looked shocked for a minute, but he quickly snapped into action. "Have you got the pin?"

"Yes." Libby pointed to her chest.

He hurried into the adjoining dentist's office and reached behind the cabinet. His hand came out with the flag rolled around its stick. "Okay. We're in the right place. We've got the flag and the pin. We need the mirror. Let's go."

Libby followed him out the door and he trotted down the wooden sidewalk until they came to the entrance to The Fashion Shoppe.

"It's in here. In the corner," he whispered.

Libby peered through the window, past the dress and hat and purse on display. "The lights are on, but it doesn't look like anyone's there."

"Mrs. Paavoneimi's probably gone to see what's happening, like everyone else. Let's get it."

As they entered the shop a bell jangled above the door. They stopped still in their tracks waiting to see if anyone would come through the curtain at the back of the shop. No one did. Nathan went right to the mirror. "Get the other end," he ordered. Together they balanced the mirror and its stand. Libby backed her end out of the shop door and they slowly carried the mirror up the street. It was heavy and awkward; the mirror kept trying to swing out. So it took longer than Libby hoped to haul it back to the doctors' offices.

They set it down on the wooden sidewalk, near the street edge. "I think this is about where we were," Libby said.

"I don't think so," Nathan replied. "I remember there was a knot in a board I was laying on."

"Knot – snot," Libby grumbled as Nathan got down on his hands and knees and crawled across the boards looking for a knot he recognized. Libby chewed on her thumb. "Hurry. Hurry," she begged, keeping an eye on the corner where people might cross coming back from the Italian Hall.

"Here it is!" he shouted. "Get the flag."

Libby retrieved the flag, trying to remember exactly what had happened, what had been said and done and in what order back in the school storage room.

They stood on the wooden sidewalk, mirror stand centered over a certain knot on a certain board that Nathan was sure was the right one. Libby unrolled the flag.

"Ready? We've got to fight and crash into the mirror, right?" Nathan said, making a grab for the flag.

"It's not that easy, Nathan. We have to do it exactly the

same. I'm trying to remember. Use your big brain and help me. I had the flag and you grabbed it and you said you could use this. Right?"

"Okay. I'll say that. Are we ready?"

"No. Then I said, 'No, you can't have it. It's mine. It's Annie's.' That's when we started fighting over it. I said, 'Let go!' and you said......."

'Make me, Bean-brain.' I'm starting to remember it all now. Then you twirled around and wrapped yourself all up in the flag. I said, 'Hey, cut it out.' But it was too late. We fell into the mirror, and VOILA! Here we were."

"Right. I think that's it."

"Okay. Let's go," he said again.

Libby looked at Nathan, from his shoes to his tall socks and short pants, to the floppy white shirt that wasn't so white any more. But all she could see was the collar and a strip down the center front. "The jackets, Nathan! We've got to get rid of these jackets." They shrugged them off and ran back into the dentist's office and put them back on the hooks they'd come from.

Back on the street again, Nathan said, "Okay, can we do it now?"

"I think so," Libby said. She hoped so.

Nathan grabbed the flag and they began a slow motion tug-of-war tussle with it. Nathan said, "I could use this."

Libby said, "No. You can't. It's mine. It's Annie's. Let go!"

Nathan said, "Make me, bean-brain."

Libby began to roll herself up in the flag. Then she stopped. "Wait!"

"Now what?" Nathan was exasperated.

"Something still doesn't seem right. We're forgetting something."

"I can't remember anything else."

"Wait a minute." Libby chewed on the side of her thumb some more, thinking. C'mon, brain, she said to herself. Here's your chance to prove you're gifted and talented. Think. Think. She took deep breaths, head down, watching her chest move in and out. She remembered the eyes, the sad eyes in the mirror. She knew now whose eyes they were and why they were so sad. And she remembered how she had held the copper leaf pin and moved it in and out from her chest as the eyes in the mirror changed. That was it!

"Nathan, I've got it! The last thing I forgot. I wasn't wearing the pin. It was in my hand."

Nathan grinned as she unclasped the pin from the pleat on the front of her dress and clutched it in her hand. "You know, I'm beginning to think you don't have a bean brain, after all. I would never have remembered that. We'd have never gotten home."

"Well," Libby said charitably, "I wouldn't have been able to find the mirror. So I guess we need each other."

"Now can we go?" Nathan asked once more.

Libby nodded. "Yes. It feels right this time. Let's do it."

Nathan grabbed the flag. "I could use this," he said.

"Oh, no, you can't. It's mine! It's Annie's! Let go!"

"Make me, Bean-brain."

Libby clutched the pin to her chest as she twirled herself into the flag. For one quick moment she had the strangest feeling, like she was being pulled, dizzily in two different directions. Then Nathan's weight crashed into her. A hot sharpness stabbed her chest and she fell into blackness.

Chapter 21

"Ow! Get off me," Libby moaned. She was trapped again in the cocoon of the flag, with Nathan's weight pinning her down. He lay crosswise over the top of her, his head about eight inches away from hers. His eyes were closed and he was still. But Libby could feel his breath on her face, so she didn't have to worry that he might be dead. She was close enough and he was quiet enough for her to count his freckles. If she had a pen, and if she could move her hands and arms, she could connect the dots of his freckles and see what kind of picture his face would make. But the only part of her body that she could move was her neck – a little. She counted freckles until she got to sixty-eight. What a dumb thing to be doing right now, she told herself. A gifted and talented person would be trying to find out if they'd made it back to the present. So she tried to stretch and swivel her neck and head from side to side. Soon, instead of resting on her right ear, she was resting on the back of her head. Now she could see something besides Nathan's face.

Did it work? Had they come back? Libby looked directly up. A dim, round, orangey light shone right into her eyes. It was too small to be the copper moon. By swerving her eyes sideways she could see tall metal shelves, crowded with boxes, rising up on either side of her like skyscrapers. Yes! It sure looked like the school storeroom, even though she had never seen it before from this ant's eye view. The air was dusty and Libby felt a tickle in her nose. She sneezed a mighty sneeze and Nathan stirred.

She turned her head back toward him. "Nathan! Wake up. Get off me. I can hardly breathe. Nathan!" She yelled his name and his eyes began to flutter open. He moaned and opened his eyes completely to look at her. He blinked twice.

"Get off me, please," she begged.

"What? Oh, sure." He rolled off her and sat up, rubbing his head.

"Help me get out of this flag," Libby asked. He helped her unroll from the flag's clutches.

A puzzled frown creased his face. "Boy, I must have really bumped my head. I think I was unconscious. I was having the strangest dream. And you were in it. You and your hero, Big Annie."

"Nathan, it wasn't a dream. We were in Calumet. It was 1913. Christmas time. We traveled through time."

"Right," Nathan said, sneering. "Like I'm going to believe that? You're nuts."

"It's true," she said. How could she convince him? "Listen, could both of us have had the exact same dream?"

"Not likely."

"Did you dream that you had a job, being a delivery boy for a Dr. Westerberg?"

"How'd you know?"

"I told you. We were both there. In the past."

Nathan shook his head hard in disbelief.

"Did you spend your quarters on bread and nut meal and jam and penny candy at an A&P grocery story?"

Nathan nodded. "You're weirding out on me," he said, voice unsure.

"Did you go to the Italian Hall and did you eat chocolate drops there?"

Nathan nodded again. But still he could not believe it. "It's just a coincidence. We must have both bumped our heads the same way. I mean, time travel is not a scientific possibility. Quantum physics hasn't figured that out yet. No. Uh-uh. No way. It was a dream."

"Nathan, the Italian Hall disaster really happened, I'll prove it to you when I finish my research. We were there. I don't care if it's scientifically provable or not. It happened, " Libby said with emphasis.

"But....," Nathan was thinking it over. Libby could almost see his mind working, trying to figure it out, make it make sense.

"Nathan, would you believe it if I showed you something from the past?"

"If you could prove it actually was from the past, which I don't think is possible, then maybe."

"Check your pockets."

Nathan stuck his hands into both large pockets of his baggy knee pants. When he pulled his hands out each of them held a small paper sack. He set one sack down on the floor. He opened the other and peered inside.

Libby watched his fingers and then his eyes. His fingers reached into the sack and came out with a clump of chocolate drops, squashed together into a brown and white glob. His eyes opened so wide with amazement that they were almost complete circles. Like an owl face, Libby thought. "You know there is only one place those chocolate drops could have come from, don't you? Only one way they could have gotten into your pockets. You put them there while you were in the kitchen at the Italian Hall."

Nathan nodded slowly, dazed. "I....I guess so," he stammered.

Libby gave him a sassy grin and slapped her hand down hard on his back. "Welcome back to the present," she said. She made her ferret face. "Let's go. I've got some research to do to find out what happened after we left Calumet."

Nathan followed her meekly. For the first time he didn't rush and push to be first, to out-do her. If he stays this way, Libby thought, maybe we can become friends in the present, the way we were in the past. She hoped so. She had a lot of freckles still to count.

Epilogue

Libby stood in the center of the stage in the school auditorium, trying to remember her posture, Big Annie's posture. She wore her newly laundered white ruffled dress. On the pleats that ran down the front of the dress she had pinned her copper leaf pin right over her heart. Mom had used lots of pins and combs and things, plus a half a can of hair spray to coax her hair into a knot at the back of her head.

In the audience, seated on folding chairs sat the principal, the teachers, the P.T.A., and the families of the History Alive! kids. They listened intently. Libby was nearly at the end of her presentation as Big Annie Clemenc of Calumet.

She stopped to take a breath and try her half–teeth Annie smile. So far, so good, she thought as she caught Ms. Sullivan's eye. Ms. Sullivan raised her hand and gave Libby the thumbs up sign. She took another breath and reminded herself that she was a gifted and talented person, and that she was acting as Big Annie.

"...........So, seventy three people, fifty eight of them children, died that horrible Christmas Eve at the Italian Hall. There was no fire. Panic killed them. And no one ever found out who yelled "Fire!" It's an unsolved mystery.

*"After that, all the heart went out of the strike.
What was there left to strike for, people said. The
men went back to work in the mines. It was over.
But it will never be over for me, even now when I
am an old woman.*

*"I left Calumet, left my husband, and went with
Frank Shavs, the journalist who reported on the
strike for the Chicago Newspapers. I have spent
the rest of my life as his wife.*

*"The newspapers printed my picture. Even in
New York. They called me a hero and a saint. But I
wasn't. I did things that a saint would never do.
And I did nothing to be a hero. I only wanted to
help the miners and their families have a better life.*

*"But my life? For all these years, even far away
from Calumet, I have been haunted by the ghosts
of the children, by the ghosts of better times.
And that's the truth of my life."*

Libby stopped, bowed her head slightly, and left the
stage as her ears filled with applause. She lifted her eyes
and whispered, "The applause is for you, Annie, not for
me." She ran off the stage to collect her mom's hug. It
had been an exciting adventure, but she would be glad to
get out of her Annie dress, glad to be Libby Larson again,
in her jeans and pink Las Vegas tee shirt.

Sources

BOOKS:
Lankton, Larry. Cradle to Grave. Life, Work, and Death at the Lake Superior Copper Mines. 1991. Oxford University Press. New York.

Stanley, Jerry. Big Annie of Calumet. 1996. Crown Publishers. New York.

Thurner, Arthur W. Rebels on the Range. 1984. Crown Publishers. New York.

Thurner, Arthur W. Strangers and Sojourners. A History of Michigan's Keweenaw Peninsula. 1994. Wayne State University Press. Detroit, MI.

PERIODICALS:
Andrews, Clarence A. "Big Annie and the 1913 Michigan Copper Strike."
MICHIGAN HISTORY. Vol. 57. Spring 1973.

Wendland, Michael F. "The Calumet Tragedy."
AMERICAN HERITAGE.
April-May 1986.

Other sources:
County coroner's report
Newspaper accounts
Copper Country Archives, Michigan Technological University

Author's Notes

The search for historical accuracy in the story of the Italian Hall tragedy is a difficult one. Urban legends have grown up around the event. Twenty "eye-witnesses" gave twenty different accounts of what actually happened. Coroner's reports and sheriff's reports sometimes conflict. I have tried to portray the events as true to historical fact as I could determine. Annie Clemenc did exist. The part she played in the strike, the parades, and the Italian Hall party are all true. There are, however, because of the nature of time-travel fiction, made-up characters. Libby and Nathan do not exist except in my imagination. The Westerberg doctors and Libby's family members, including her grandfather Oscar and his relationship to Annie, are also gleaned only from my imagination. The doctors' offices do exist. You can visit them in Calumet. There's a bicycle shop there now. Although Oscar did not exist, the isolation of people from others of different nationalities and religions is true of that time.

I want to thank the members of my writing group in the Upper Peninsula Writing Project whose support and suggestions helped me enormously. I am indebted to my long-time mentor, Judy Parlato, who is a terrific editor. If I thanked him all day it would not be sufficient thanks to my husband Bill who allows me to live in the past even when the house needs cleaning, the laundry needs doing, and he needs attention in the present. Thanks also to the children and their teachers who read my books, act them out, and, best of all, write letters to me about them. Thanks a bunch!

Anna Clemenc, "Big Annie," with her flag.

Above: Women marching to support the copper miners' strike.

The Italian Hall in mourning on December 25, 1913. Note the flag at half-mast.

The Italian Hall in Mourning, the Next Day After Disaster

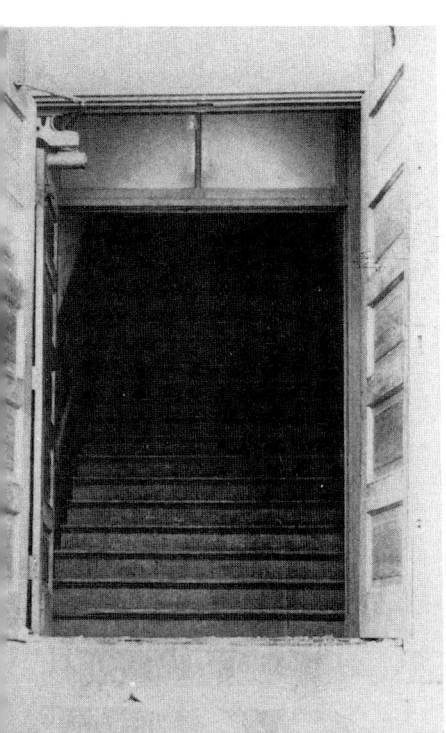

The stairs to the Italian Hall.

Below: The Italian Hall the morning after the tragedy, 12-25-13.

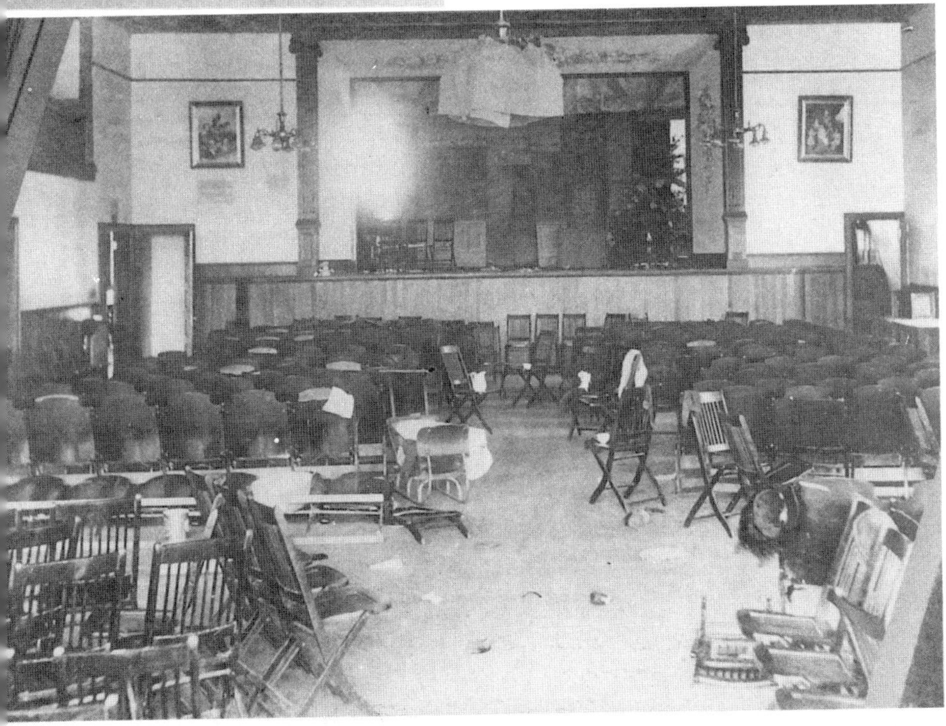

Photos from the collection of the Michigan Technological University Archives & Copper Country Historical Collections

The Italian Hall Memorial Park, Calumet, MI. The arched doorway from the building.

Some of the plaques at the Italian Hall Memorial, Calumet, MI.